BRAINFOOD
Nutrition and Your Brain

Brian L.G. Morgan, Ph.D. and Roberta Morgan

The Body Press
Tucson, Arizona

THE BODY PRESS
A division of HPBooks, Inc.
575 East River Road
Tucson, Arizona 85704

Library of Congress Cataloging-in-Publication Data

Morgan, Brian L. G.
  Brainfood : nutrition and your brain.

  Bibliography: p.
  Includes index.
  1. Brain.   2. Nutrition.   3. Mental health.
I. Morgan, Roberta, 1953-   .   II. Title.
QP376.M62   1987   612'.82   87-6389
ISBN 0-89586-565-3
ISBN 0-89586-558-0 (pbk.)

10 9 8 7 6 5 4 3 2 1
First Printing

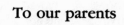
To our parents

Acknowledgments

There are many people to thank for their help and cooperation in the preparation of this book. We would like to especially thank; Glenn Cowley, a supportive agent and good friend; Cynthia Merman and Sam Mitnick, two fine editors, for their patience and assistance in shaping this project; Dr. Myron Winick, for his support through the years; Britt Bell, for first believing in the concept; and all the fine researchers in this field whose work has contributed so much both to our own research and to the whole of society.

Contents

List of Tables

List of Figures

(Illustrations by Lauren Keswick.
Art direction and conceptualization by John W. Karapelou of the Audio-Visual Service,
College of Physicians and Surgeons. Columbia University, New York.)

PREFACE

Everything you are doing at this moment, on opening this book, is being controlled or regulated by your brain. That this is true of reading is perhaps obvious, but it also holds true for all subsidiary activities. Are you crossing your legs, rubbing your eyes, settling back in the chair to get more comfortable? The brain is in control of all these movements—even your breathing is being carefully regulated by your brain. during every minute of the day and night, even when you are fast asleep, your brain is thinking, deciding, judging. It determines your every mood, every physical action, every bodily reaction.

Most of us realize that the kind of food we eat has a lot to do with our well-being. We know that too much (combined with not enough exercise) makes us fat; that a deficiency of vitamin D or calcium during childhood results in soft bones and the deformed limbs of rickets. Fewer of us are aware, however, of the ways in which nutrition specifically affects the brain, and consequently, not only the body's functions controlled by the brain, but behavior and mental health as well. In the following pages we deal with such common problems as insomnia, appetite control, depression, lethargy, senility, loss of memory, and female menstrual irregularities. Each of these complaints is affected by the balance or imbalance of certain brain chemicals; in each case the proper diet, or the addition of specific nutrients to the diet, can help alleviate the condition.

By learning about what foods and specific dietary substances affect the brain, you will find out ways to minimize mood swings, eat less, sleep better. learn more quickly, and remember more of what you learn. Menstrual irregularities and minor depressions can be significantly eased. And many of the memory problems affecting older people can also be erased through the proper "brain food" diet.

One young woman with chronic sleeping problems found that by eating snacks high in carbohydrates one half hour before bedtime, her rest became normal and undisturbed for the first time since childhood. A middle-aged lawyer with a heavy workload discovered that eating a high protein lunch made him far more efficient in the afternoon. An older housewife suffering from lethargy and slight depression found her answer in tyrosine supplements.

Of course, no dietary chage is a cure, and in cases of severe illness nutritional adjustments alone may not help all that much. But it is important to realize that even though changes in the diet cannot cure all ailments, poor eating habits will adversely affect every condition, no matter how severe or how slight. If you are taking drugs to control depression, you should avoid foods likely to exacerbate your condition if you are diligently trying to lose weight it makes sense not to eat foods that make you feel hungry.

This book shows how what you eat affects your brain, and how specific foods can maintain or restore your mental and physical equilibrium. It teaches you how to deal with specific problems arising out of brain chemical imbalances. and how, by eating a correctly balanced diet for the mind, you can live both a healthier *and* a happier life. In the case of nutrition for the brain, you *are* what you eat!

B.L.G.M. & R.E.M.
New York

PART ONE

The Brain
Structure, Function, and Food

CHAPTER ONE

The Basics of Brain

Before we explain exactly how nutrition affects the brain, you should know a little about the brain itself, and how it operates.

What Does It Look Like?

The human brain is pinkish-gray in color and has a jellylike consistency. In adults it usually weighs between 1,250 and 1,400 grams. Its average size differs between the sexes and among races, but unless it falls beneath 1,000 grams, brain weight appears to have no bearing on a person's intelligence. Geniuses have been found to have tiny brains (that of the novelist Anatole France weighed less than 1,000 grams), and some mentally impaired people have abnormally large brains.

The ratio of brain to body size seems to be a better gauge of intelligence, at least among species—ours is surpassed only by the dolphin's (we are not yet sure what this indicates about dolphins). The surface area of the brain may be a more telling indicator of intelligence among species. Our brains are more deeply wrinkled and hence have a bigger surface area than those of any other animal.

Structure and Function

The major structures of the brain, and their functions—the tasks they usually perform. are summarized in Appendix 2. Take a quick look now—but don't try to memorize it; we tell you what you need to know as we go along. You can see at once that complicated reactions and emotions are often handled by more than one area; not so immediately evident is the fact that though brain tissue, once damaged, cannot be regenerated, some parts of the brain may be able to take over the jobs of other parts in cases of accident or injury.

On the surface, the brain appears to have the property of bilateral symmetry, that is, like our bodies, it has two matching parts. We would suspect that our left brain does the same things as our right one, just as our left kidney or lung performs the same function as our right one does. And indeed, in terms of the input we get from our nerves, which supply information to the brain about our bodies, and that part of our brain's output which causes the movement of muscles, the operation of the two hemispheres does follow a simple symmetrical pattern: each side of the brain is primarily concerned with the opposite side of the body. The muscles of the right hand and foot are controlled by the left cortex. Information coming from the right side of the body goes mainly to the left side of the brain. The distribution of signals from the eyes generally follows the same pattern: the images you see from the right half of space in both eyes are projected onto the left visual cortex, and the left half of visual space goes to the right cortex.

Although the sensory and motor functions of the two hemispheres are indeed symmetrical, the distribution of the more specialized functions of the brain is quite different. The left side of the cerebral cortex controls speech; the right side governs melodies. Thus, people with damage to the left hemisphere may not be able to speak clearly or remember verbal material, but they can still sing. And they can still draw solid objects, recall spatial locations, faces. and abstract visual patterns, though they may have difficulty with writing, calculating, and logic, as well as speech.

One of the most surprising recent findings is that emotion and "state of mind" are associated with the cerebral cortex, the thinking part of the brain, and particularly with the right hemisphere. Injuries to parts of the left hemisphere are accompanied by feelings of loss that might be expected to follow any serious injury. The patient is disturbed by his disability and is often extremely depressed. However, damage done to most areas of the right hemisphere tends to leave the patient completely unconcerned about his changed condition, and to impair as well his ability to recognize emotional changes in other people: although understanding the meaning of what is said to him, for example, he may fail to see that it is being said in an angry or humorous way.

Brain Structure at the Micro Level

The Neurons

The units that make up our nervous systems are called *neurons*, or nerve cells. They are designed to communicate constantly with one another. There are about 50 billion neurons in the cerebral cortex, 40 billion more in the cerebellum, and another 10 billion in the remaining structures of the brain and spinal cord—about the same number as there are stars in our galaxy.

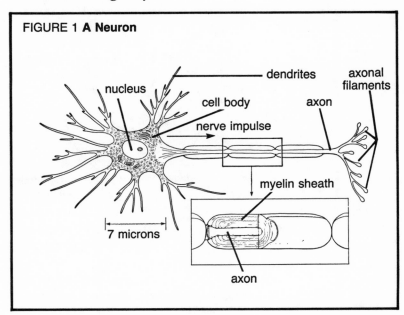

FIGURE 1 **A Neuron**

Each neuron receives and transmits messages through the thousands of filaments—called *axons* and *dendrites*—that link it to other neurons. The axon transmits signals from the nerve cell's body to other cells across narrow junctions known as *synapses*.

Signals pass along nerve cells electrically, as they would along a wire, and chemical substances (called *neurotransmitters*) pass messages across the synaptic gap between one cell and the next. Some axons link nearby regions of nerve tissue; others send signals to and receive signals from remote areas of the body. Dendrites (which look like little trees) are networks of short fibers that branch out from the cell's body and receive impulses, primarily across synapses, from the axons of other neurons. A typical neuron can have anywhere from 1,000 to 10,000 synapses (connections). (In this closely interconnecting network, although synapses are most often between the axon of one cell and the dendrite of another, there are also synaptic junctions between axon and axon, between dendrite and dendrite, and between axon and cell body.)

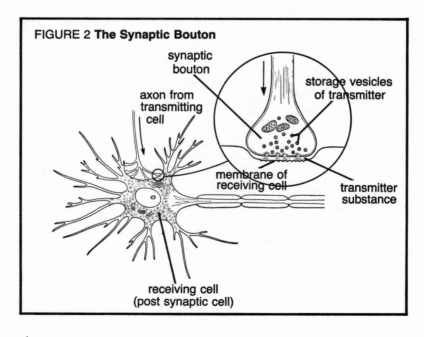

FIGURE 2 **The Synaptic Bouton**

synaptic bouton

axon from transmitting cell

storage vesicles of transmitter

membrane of receiving cell

transmitter substance

receiving cell (post synaptic cell)

The cell bodies of the neurons and the dendrites are clustered together in regions of the brain called *gray matter* because they appear gray in color.

Nerve Pathways

If you cut open a human brain and look at it under a microscope, it will appear to be meaningless mesh of neurons. Yet a speeding signal through the nervous system manages to find the exact area of the brain designed to handle that specific type of signal. That region also sends out instructions that reach only specific muscles. All of this is possible because our brains are built somewhat like telephone exchanges, with nerve fibers functioning as wiring and special neuron centers acting as the switchboards, controlling the signals that are flowing in or out.

Some of these special centers, such as the cerebral cortex or the cerebellum, are large enough to be seen by the naked eye. Others, including those hidden in the brainstem, are clusters of cells so small that you need a microscope to see them. The maze of "wires" between these switchboards consists mostly of ordered bundles of nerve fibers known as *tracts*. Each tract is made up of axons from cell bodies located in one "switchboard" that end at one or more of the other "switchboards."

These nerves may be divided into two main groups: those making up the *somatic* (bodily) nervous system and those making up the *autonomic* (self-regulating) nervous system. The somatic system is composed of two kinds of nerves: *motor nerves* make a muscle act on orders from the brain or spinal cord; *sensory nerves* work in the opposite way, bringing information to the brain and spinal cord from sensors in the skin, eyes, tongue, nostrils, joints, and muscles. Subconsciously bombarded by this constant artillery of sensory information coming in, we use the knowledge it brings us about our posture and surroundings to control how we hold ourselves or move around. In other words, sensory nerves tell the brain what needs to be done, and the brain then tells the motor nerves what to do and how to do it.

The autonomic nervous system controls our glands, and structures like our heart, lungs, blood vessels, and the pupils of our eyes. All this is usually beyond our conscious control. We don't have to remember to breathe—our autonomic nervous system—automatically—takes care of it.

Glial Cell

Neurons are not the only type of cells found in the brain. Several kinds of noncommunicating cells, called *glial cells*, support, nourish, and insulate the neurons, outnumbering them 10 to 1. Unlike the neurons, glial cells do not generate electrical impulses. But they play a vital role in the passage of information along the nerve network. A substance called *myelin* is laid down around some neurons in a spiral fashion by a particular type of glial cell, and axons covered by this myelin sheath conduct impulses up to 12 times faster than those without it.

The areas of the brain containing myelinated axons are called "white matter" because these axons appear white in color.

The Synapse and Neurotransmitters

When a signal entering the brain or going from one brain cell to another arrives at the synapse at the end of an axon, it causes certain *neurotransmitters* to be released. These chemicals burst forth from tiny sacs at the end of the axons. The neurotransmitters cross the narrow synaptic gap between their axon and the adjacent inactive neuron's cell body or dendrites, and lock onto places conducive to them (called *receptor sites*) in that neuron's cell membrane. The receiving cell is activated and it transmits the message to the appropriate part of the brain.

These neurotransmitters -including *acetylcholine* (found in several parts of the brain), *norepinephrine* (found in the brainstem, hypothalmus, and limbic system), *serotonin*, and *epinephrine*—are appropriately called *excitatory* neurotransmitters. There are also *inhibitory* neurotransmitters—like *gamma aminobutyric acid* or *GABA* (found in the brain's outer gray matter), *glycine* (found in the spinal cord), and *Substance P*—that block electrical impulses and stop messages from moving any further. At any one instant, one brain cell may receive thousands of contradictory signals from the other brain cells with which it is in contact. Whether or not it sends a message, or what kind of a message it sends, depends on how many signals of each kind it receives. In addition, there are *endorphins* and *enkephalins*. These are not neurotransmitters in the true sense, but they affect our emotions, appetite and feelings of pain. Thus they are crucial to our discussion.

The Major Neurotransmitters and Their Functions

Neurons that carry out the same functions contain the same kind of neurotransmitter. For example, all those responsible for moving your muscles contain acetylcholine, all those responsible for feelings of hunger contain norepinephrine, and all those involved in making you feel sleepy contain serotonin.

There are perhaps as many as 70 different neurotransmitters in your brain. For the purposes of this book, we examine only those ten which most obviously influence our moods, reactions, and everyday life.

Neurotransmitters are made from the protein in the food we eat. Protein is first broken down in our stomach and intestine into its constituent molecules, called *amino acids*. The amino acids then pass into our bloodstream, our brain absorbs them from the blood flow, and uses them to make neurotransmitters.

The relative levels of neurotransmitters in your brain is crucial to its proper operation. Here we encounter the concept of balance. This balance or lack of balance is a result of the levels of nutrients in your blood, which are regulated by your daily diet. Any deficiencies in nutrients will reduce the levels of certain neurotransmitters and thus adversely affect the types of behavior they are responsible for. Conversely, a physical or mental problem can be corrected by boosting the level of the particular neurotransmitter that affects it, and this can be done by making a simple alteration in the composition of your diet. As an example of why this whole issue of relative balance among neurotransmitters is so important, let's look at the mechanisms behind the regulation of appetite.

Norepinephrine release is one of the main factors that control feelings of hunger. The level of norepinephrine helps

determine whether or how you feel hungry. If your norepinephrine levels are too low, you may not feel hungry even if
you have not eaten for days. On the other hand, if the levels are
too high, you may constantly feel hungry, even after a big meal.
In the course of a normal day, these levels fluctuate to tell you
when to eat and when not to. But if something goes wrong
with this mechanism, either because of an unbalanced diet, a
physical illness, or an emotional upset, problems like obesity
(if the levels stay too high) or anorexia nervosa (if the levels
stay too low) can result.

So, in treating disorders like over- and undereating, it is
important to realize that the composition of the foods eaten is
almost as important as the amount. If you eat a lot of foods that

Table 1. Neurotransmitters

Excitatory Neurotransmitters

Neurotransmitter	Function
Acetylcholine	Affects short-term memory, feelings of thirst, and body temperature. Deficiencies can cause memory problems and *minor* senility.
Epinephrine	Affects survival instinct—the "fight or flight" response during a crisis. It is also known as *adrenaline.*
Norepinephrine	Affects long-term memory and feelings of hunger. Deficiencies can result in the type of depression known as lethargy (a lack of interest in anything), and a loss of appetite.
Serotonin	Affects the emotions, sleeping habits, and satiety (the absence of hunger). Deficiencies can cause nonpsychotic depression, insomnia. disturbances in the appetite, and a lowered pain tolerance.

tell the brain to make norepinephrine, the levels will be high, and you could feel hungry all the time—a situation you wouldn't want if you were on a diet. The opposite situation would be detrimental to people who are trying to gain weight.

Different neurotransmitters are manufactured by different nutrients in the diet. Too much or too little of one or more nutrients can cause neurotransmitter levels to fluctuate abnormally, and the type of behavior they affect can be disturbed. In the following chapters, we discuss which types of foods affect which neurotransmitters, and, therefore, which types of behavior. We also tell you how to adjust your diet to achieve the emotional and behavioral effects you desire.

Inhibitory Neurotransmitters

Neurotransmitter	Function
Endorphins (stronger form) Enkephalins (weaker form)	The brain's natural painkillers or opiates; secretion of them yields reduction in feelings of pain. Enkephalins are produced throughout the brain tissues. Endorphins are made by the pituitary gland and hypothalmus and they also have a effect on appetite and emotions. Exercise. as well as chronic pain result in the release of these chemicals, which is why exercise has been linked to both pain reduction and appetite control.
Gamma-aminobutyric Acid (GABA)	The main inhibitory transmitter in the brain, GABA slows down the rate at which certain messages pass. Without it, our movements would be jerky and somewhat uncontrollable.
Substance P	Signals pain to the brain.
Glycine	Another inhibitory transmitter.

Table 2

Pituitary Hormones

Hormone	Function
Adrenocorticotropin (ACTH)	Controls the adrenal glands, which give us energy.
Follicle stimulating hormone (FSH)	Works on the ovaries and testes.
Growth hormone (GH)	Promotes normal growth.
Luteinizing hormone (LH)	Acts on the ovaries (appears only in women).
Melanocyte stimulating hormone (MSH)	Stimulates the production of pigment in the skin, as when you get a suntan.
Oxytocin	Works on the breasts and uterus.
Prolactin	Works on the breasts (in women only).
Thyroid stimulating hormone (TSH)	Regulates the thyroid gland, which affects growth and metabolism.
Vasopressin	Acts upon the kidneys.

The rate of secretion of seven of the pituitary hormones is controlled by a corresponding hormone in the hypothalamus and the pituitary controls the other two.

Hormones

The brain also contains a variety of *hormones*, chemical messengers made out of proteins that are secreted by the body's *endocrine glands*. Hormones control the rate and way in which various reactions in the body occur. For our purposes we need to look at only the two hormone-secreting glands in

Table 3

Hypothalamic Hormone

Hormone	Function
Corticotropin-releasing hormone, TSH-releasing hormone, GH-releasing hormone, FSH/LH-releasing hormone	Promote the release of ACTH, TSH, GH, and FSH and LH respectively.
Somatostatin, prolactin release inhibitory hormone, and MSH-release inhibitory hormone (MIH)	Inhibit the release of GH and TSH, prolactin, and MSH respectively.

the brain—the pituitary and the hypothalamus.

The pituitary gland secretes nine hormones into the bloodstream each of which controls a targeted tissue in the body.

The hormones secreted by the hypothalamus are very sensitive to the body's local and immediate needs. Say you work late one night at the office and on your way home you sense that someone is following you. As you speed up your steps, the footsteps behind you also accelerate. Your brain perceives the stressful and possibly dangerous situation and relays to your hypothalamus the order to secrete corticotropin-releasing hormone into your bloodstream. Your hypothalamus and pituitary are directly connected by blood vessels and when this hormone reaches the pituitary. ACTH is secreted. ACTH passes into your bloodstream, and eventually ends up in your adrenal glands where it causes the release of adrenalin, which protects your body against the stressful situation by invoking the "fight-or-flight" response. Your blood pressure rises, more blood flows to your muscles. and your energy level is stimulated. You are totally alert, stronger, and quicker—in other words, more able to deal with the situation. You now have the energy to outrun your potential attacker and make it safely home.

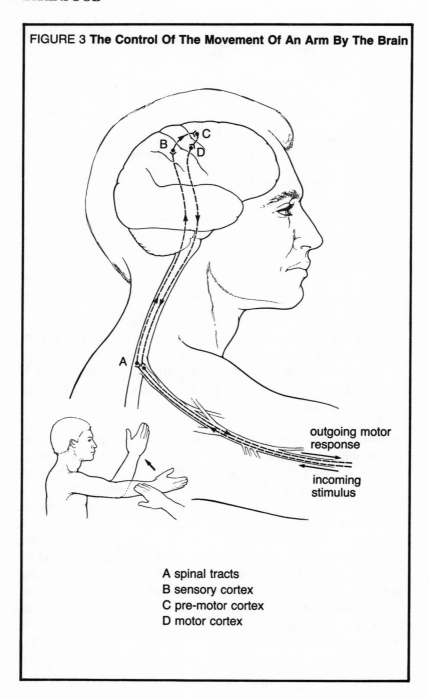

FIGURE 3 **The Control Of The Movement Of An Arm By The Brain**

outgoing motor response

incoming stimulus

A spinal tracts
B sensory cortex
C pre-motor cortex
D motor cortex

Following a Message

To see how all the systems of the brain operate, let's follow one message as it moves through this intricate machinery.

Someone touches you on the arm. This creates an electrical impulse in the dendrites of the nerve touched. This impulse is transmitted along the axon to the cell body of the sensory neuron in the spinal cord (sensory neurons have axons at each end of their cell bodies). The axon going out of the sensory neuron conveys this impulse to the filaments at its end. This releases the appropriate neurotransmitters, and the axon forms connections across the synapses with a number of other neurons. These neurons are the ones that alert the different areas of the brain that affect movement, in particular the *sensory cortex*, the *premotor cortex*, and the *motor cortex*.

The sensory cortex interprets bodily sensations—wet/dry, hot/ cold, pain/pleasure. Its neurons connect with neurons passing to the premotor cortex, the part of the brain that plans what type of action is needed in light of what it has done in the past in a similar situation. One or more of the premotor neurons are made to excite adjacent neurons in the motor

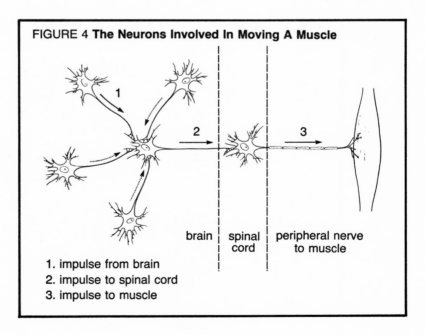

FIGURE 4 **The Neurons Involved In Moving A Muscle**

brain | spinal | peripheral nerve
cord | to muscle

1. impulse from brain
2. impulse to spinal cord
3. impulse to muscle

cortex, which puts into effect the decision of the premotor cortex either to "move" or "not move." Motor neurons are then excited. Their message is transmitted down their axons to the brainstem to connect with neurons that send instructions to the muscles. These directions will be either to "act" or "not act.) These same neurons also receive input from other parts of the brain, controlling and smoothing out the movement of the muscle in question—the one being touched.

It is remarkable to think that all this takes place easily, effortlessly, and automatically in a fraction of a second. The brain conducts millions of such interchanges every day. Because it does these things so automatically, we tend to take it for granted, believe it will always function normally no matter what, and sometimes even abuse it by not giving it what it needs. The next chapter describes in general terms what your brain needs to function well. Subsequent chapters discuss the necessary brain foods to ensure peak physical, mental, and emotional performance.

CHAPTER TWO

Nutrition for Brain Operation, Maintenance, and Repair

The Brain's Need for Energy—A Few Facts

What does the brain need to keep it operating smoothly and efficiently? More than anything else, it needs energy. A light bulb will dim if the current is reduced, will go out completely if the current is cut off. The same is true for the brain. Energy must be there at all times—and in the right quantities—or malfunctions will occur. The brain will become "dimmer," and emotional or physical problems will result.

This energy comes mainly from the food we eat. The brain's enormously complex circuitry is always "turned on" and so requires constant fuel for its operation and maintenance. Furthermore, the brain can store very little in the way of nutrients needed to satisfy its energy needs. So knowing exactly what to eat for brain maintenance, operation, repair, and growth—and eating it every day—will ensure our total mental health.

The Brain Electric
The transmission of signals along nerves depends on the

movement of electrically charged particles called *ions*, which are found in the fluids both inside and around the body's cells, including the neurons. The flow of these ions constitutes an electrical current. The brain is constantly generating about 25 watts of electricity, enough to light a small room!

Neurons have active mechanisms (which means that they use energy continuously) called *sodium pumps*. When the nerve cells are resting, these pumps keep the insides of the cells negatively charged and the areas outside of the cell membrane positively charged. A typical small neuron can have as many as one million sodium pumps.

When a neuron is stimulated, as when light comes into your eyes when you open them in the morning, the nerve membrane lets in, or becomes permeable to, electrically positive sodium ions. When these sodium ions begin their flow into the cell, they cause the first area they encounter in the cell to become electrically positive. This increases the permeability of that section of cell membrane and hence more sodium ions enter until that area becomes as positive as it can be. Now the ions move from this first positive area to the next area, making

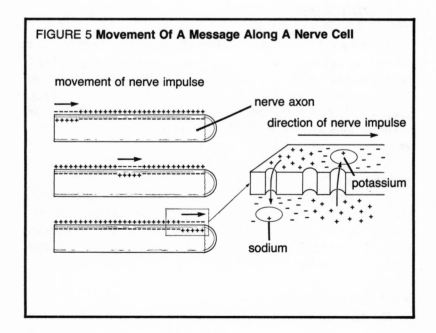

FIGURE 5 **Movement Of A Message Along A Nerve Cell**

movement of nerve impulse

nerve axon

direction of nerve impulse

potassium

sodium

it less negative. The membrane of this area becomes permeable to sodium ions, and so on, until eventually the entire neuron, all the way down the axon, is positive. The areas of reversed charges are called *nerve impulses.*

But the message must pass so that the nerve can return to its resting state and be ready to receive and pass on another message. So a split second after the nerve cell membrane becomes permeable to sodium ions, it becomes permeable as well to potassium. Potassium is another positively charged ion, but this ion is concentrated mainly inside the cells when they are resting. As the potassium ions move outward in greater and greater numbers, the internal charge of the neuron turns relatively negative again, area by area, until it finally returns to its resting level. At this point, the nerve impulse has completely passed.

Now the sodium ions are pumped out of the cell and potassium ions back in, in order to recharge the membrane just like a battery recharger would. The pumps let out one sodium ion for every potassium ion they let in. Once the original charged state of the neuron is restored—negative on the inside, positive on the outside—the axon is ready to conduct another nerve impulse.

This entire process takes place in a fraction of a second. We are processing information constantly along our nerve networks, and reacting to sensory input in what seems to be an immediate way. We touch the fire, and instantly withdraw our hands. Yet a whole chain of nerve impulses are pulsing through our bodies and brains between the touching of that fire and the withdrawing of our hands.

Fuel for the Pump

For the sodium pumps to do their work, they must be constantly supplied with energy. The food we eat is combined with oxygen to yield carbon dioxide, water, and energy. Carbon dioxide is eliminated from the body through the lungs when we exhale. The water is excreted by the kidneys. The energy is left to run the body.

Every minute, over one-and-a-half pints of blood containing food and oxygen flow through the brain. The brain receives one-fifth of the body's total supply of blood, even though it accounts for only one-fiftieth of the body's total weight. In addition, every day the brain requires about 400 calories of energy, which is equal to one-fifth of the total food intake needed by a sedentary 130-pound woman. Most of this energy is used to drive the sodium pumps.

Our brains have to be this greedy. Since they are unable to store oxygen or energy, they depend for survival on an uninterrupted blood supply. A ten-second break in this flow can cause unconsciousness. A few minutes of oxygen starvation can transform someone into a vegetable, or even result in death.

The Role of Circulation

The function of the circulation, or blood flow, is to provide nutrients to the body and to remove the waste products of food utilization (i.e., broken-down neurotransmitters, worn-

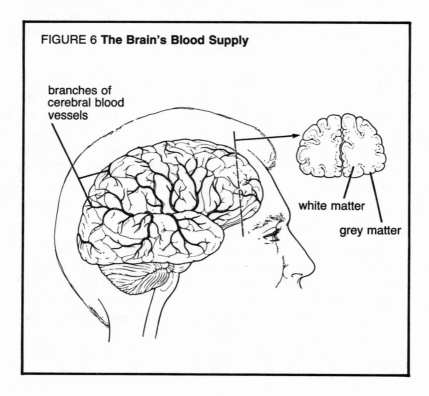

FIGURE 6 **The Brain's Blood Supply**

branches of cerebral blood vessels

white matter

grey matter

out cells). Its ability to accomplish the former job is limited or facilitated by the concentrations of nutrients in the arterial blood (the blood that goes to the brain from the heart), as well as the actual amount of blood reaching the brain. If the concentration of essential nutrients is too low, the brain will be unable to operate correctly. For example, an abnormally low oxygen level or a low level of glucose (the brain's main energy source) leads to disturbances in brain function, ranging from dizziness to confusion to unconsciousness and even to coma.

In addition, the blood flow to the brain must be kept at about 15 to 20 percent of the amount pumped out by the heart, no matter what the blood's nutrient level. A fall to half of this rate is enough to cause unconsciousness in normal, healthy people.

The Blood-Brain Barrier

Unlike most of the other organs of the body, the brain exhibits an additional property that profoundly influences its

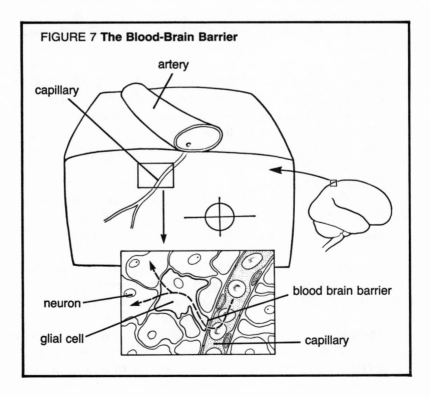

FIGURE 7 **The Blood-Brain Barrier**

artery

capillary

blood brain barrier

neuron

glial cell

capillary

nutrient supply. The blood vessels in the brain selectively exclude, retard, or quicken the transport of food substances from the blood to the brain's tissues. This phenomenon is known as the *blood brain barrier* (BBB).

Under normal circumstances the BBB protects the brain from potentially harmful substances in the blood. It also limits the number of substances the brain can use for energy; many nutrients are not allowed to cross the barrier fast enough. Lactose (the sugar found in milk) and alcohol are two substances that fall into this category.

The Role of Glucose

The brain's voracious appetite for energy continues unabated throughout the day and night. Even during sleep there is no let up in its consumption of energy—in fact, its needs may even be significantly increased during rapid eye movement (REM) sleep, or dream sleep.

Although some of this energy is used for making hormones, new cells, and proteins, as well as for making and breaking down neurotransmitters, most of it is used as mentioned—to drive the sodium pumps.

Under normal circumstances, the brain uses mainly *glucose* for energy. Glucose is a component molecule of starches and other carbohydrates, such as simple sugar (sucrose) and milk sugar (lactose) found in our diets. These sugars and starches are broken down in the mouth and intestines, where they then enter the blood via the intestinal wall. The brain absorbs this glucose from the blood, and with the aid of oxygen, the B-complex vitamins, magnesium, zinc, iron, and copper, it is "burned" (broken down) in the brain's cells to liberate the energy it contains. (The vitamins and minerals mentioned act as *cofactors*, substances that help carry out chemical reactions.)

The brain needs 110 grams of glucose every day. But a jolt of 110 grams once a day won't satisfy the brain. The brain must be constantly supplied with blood containing between 70 to 100 mg. of glucose per 100 ml. of blood. When your blood glucose levels suddenly drop to below 70 mg./100 ml., you may feel light-headed, dizzy, and can even faint. When the levels drop to 20 mg./100 ml., you can become confused due to serious brain malfunction. When they drop to 8 mg./100 ml., you will go into a coma and permanent brain damage will result unless the brain is resupplied with glucose within seconds.

There are three common situations in which the brain is deprived of glucose. The hormone *insulin* causes the cells in the body to absorb glucose from the blood—the brain does not need insulin for this purpose but all the other tissues do. If a diabetic injects himself with too much insulin, the cells throughout the body will pick up glucose from the blood at a very rapid rate, leaving little for the brain to use. An overdose of insulin, then, can knock down the glucose level of the blood to such a degree that the diabetic goes into a coma.

Blood glucose levels can also drop to a severely low level when a person suffers from *reactive hypoglycemia*. This disorder has received a lot of attention lately, but few people actually have it. When these people eat a meal that is very high in sugar, their pancreas produces so much insulin that their blood glucose levels drop to way below normal.

Finally, radical dieting for an extended period of time will adversely affect glucose levels. Your body's glucose reserves are sufficient to satisfy your brain's normal needs for only a few days. Nevertheless, even after two to three weeks of complete starvation, most people show none of the symptoms of brain dysfunction caused by glucose deprivation. How is this possible?

As the supply of glucose becomes depleted during starvation, the brain gradually adapts itself to using an alternative energy source. Starvation causes the body to break down its own fat stores, and one of the products yielded in this process is *ketone bodies*. The brain can use these ketones for energy when glucose is unavailable, and can meet up to 70 percent of its energy needs in this way. On the surface this doesn't sound so bad. The brain *is* getting energy. But the brain needs the B-complex vitamins and several minerals to enable it to derive energy from the ketone bodies. In only a few weeks on a fast the body becomes totally depleted of the B-vitamins, and in a little longer it uses up all the minerals. As long as there is some fat stored, there are ketones. But after a while they become unusable.

The problem goes deeper than this. Although the body can

switch over to using ketone bodies when there isn't enough glucose available, when the body's store of carbohydrates is used up, it begins to break down dietary protein and some of its own muscle tissue in order to meet the brain's minimum glucose requirements. During this process, the body destroys vital tissues, such as those of the heart muscle, which will not be regenerated.

The Need for Sodium and Potassium

Besides glucose, the first nutrients the brain constantly needs are sodium and potassium. Sodium (salt) is found in almost all foods. Potassium is found mainly in fruits and vegetables.

As we saw it is the exchange of sodium and potassium through the cell walls that enables the body and brain to exchange and process information and messages. If the concentration of sodium ions in the fluid surrounding the brain's cells drops to an abnormal level, the flow of sodium ions into the neurons will not happen in the normal way. Ions will move only from areas of high concentration to areas of low concentration, much like the water behind a lock in a river will move only downstream. When sodium concentrations drop severely, this reduces the movement of electrical current in the brain and causes a reduction in the amount of information the brain can receive.

Symptoms of sodium deficiency include loss of appetite, seizures, nausea, vomiting, and muscular weakness.

A sudden loss of sodium can be caused by drugs that drain the body of this nutrient, such as certain diuretics (thiazides, spironolactone, captopril).* Sodium concentrations can also drop because sodium has been diluted by an influx of too much water into the brain. This can be caused by drugs that cause the body to retain water, such as those used to reduce blood glucose levels (chlorpropamide, tolbutamide). This latter effect, known as *water intoxication,* can also occur if you drink too much water on a hot, sunny day without taking salt tablets. If the sodium concentrations are not elevated quickly, either by the administration of salt or by a reduction in water

---

*See Appendix 1, "How the Drugs You Take Can Affect Your Brain." pp. 165

intake, the brain cells will fill up with water. In severe cases this can even cause death.

A deficiency in potassium is just as dangerous. The symptoms are weakness, appetite loss, nausea, vomiting, listlessness, apprehension, and intermittent body pains. Drowsiness, stupor, and irrationality result from more serious deficiencies. All these symptoms, whether from a potassium deficiency or for any other reason, indicate that the sodium pumps in the brain are not working correctly.

Drugs that cause loss of potassium include diuretics (thiazides, furosemide, ethacrynic acid), aspirin taken in large doses, laxatives when they are abused, corticosteroids, antibiotics (gentamicin, amphotericin B), and the levodopa used to treat Parkinson's disease.

A balanced diet, which includes fruits and vegetables, is vital to everyone's brain health. But if you are taking any of the previously mentioned drugs, it is especially important for you to get these foods into your body. Sodium- and potassium-rich foods are listed on pp. 47 and 71.

The Role of Protein

All the tissues of the body, including those in the brain, are made up of protein, fat, and water. The brain needs protein to build new cells—new dendrites, replacements for worn-out myelin and worn-out glial cells—to make new hormones and enzymes, to code new information, and to manufacture new neurotransmitters. The brain cannot do any of these essential jobs unless there is an adequate supply of protein in the diet, which comes from meat, fish, beans, peas, lentils, soya products, dairy products, and eggs. (Protein-rich foods are listed in Table 5 on pp. 44.)

The protein you eat is broken down in your stomach and small intestine into *amino acid*s (its constituent molecules) and bundles of amino acids called *polypeptides*. From here these substances pass into your bloodstream. As the blood passes through your brain, the amino acids are moved inside the cells, through the action of three main transport systems made up of "carrier molecules," which form an integral part of the blood-brain barrier. One such system is for amino acids that are chemically acidic, one is for those which are basic, and the third carries the ones that are neutral (neither acidic nor basic).

Members of the same group compete with one another for entry into the brain. There are a limited number of sites on the transport carrier to be filled, just as there are only so many seats on a bus. Once these places have been taken, no more molecules can "hop aboard" and be taken across into the brain.

Amino acids are the "food" your brain uses to make neurotransmitters, the chemicals the body needs to regulate memory, appetite, moods, etc. And there is a simple cause-and-effect relationship between amino acids and neurotransmitters. To take just one example, *tryptophan* is an amino acid used by the brain to make serotonin (regulates sleep, appetite, and moods). The more tryptophan in your diet, the more serotonin in your brain, and the better the various functions controlled by serotonin. The same relationship exists between the other amino acids and neurotransmitters.

Amino acids are also used to produce 25 different *short peptides* (a few amino acids joined together in a chainlike structure). Many of these also act as neurotransmitters. For instance, the endorphins, which are involved in such actions as the modulation of pain, emotions, and feelings of pleasure, are short peptides. Another short peptide is substance P, which also modulates pain responses.

Since neurotransmitters are made from the amino acids that are the breakdown products of the protein you eat, it is easy to see how you can alter the levels of specific transmitters in your brain by changing the levels of specific amino acids, or proteins, in your diet.

The brain doesn't use amino acids only to make neurotransmitters. It also breaks them down to provide it with some energy. In addition, some amino acids replenish *enzymes* in the brain, which are responsible for carrying out its many metabolic actions necessary for keeping the body healthy. Enzymes are like catalysts; they are proteins that break apart or put together other substances in the body. Enzymes are neither changed nor destroyed in the process of doing their work and so can be used time and time again. But they are very specific in their activities. Each reaction in the brain and/or body has its own specific enzyme responsible for it.

There are hundreds of chemical reactions going on in the brain at any one instant in time, each with its own type of enzyme. All these enzymes are made from the amino acids that are produced by the digestion of the protein we eat.

Dendrites are also partially made from brain proteins. It has recently been shown that throughout our lives we are slowly but continuously making dendrites. This means that we actually become more intelligent with age, as long as our brains are healthy and free of arteriosclerosis (which reduces the brain's supply of oxygen and nutrients because of blocked arteries).

Finally, the brain uses amino acids to make its various hormones, including those of the hypothalamus and pituitary gland, which control all the other glands of the body.

Protein is obviously crucial to many important brain tasks. In cases of severe and prolonged protein deficiency, new cell and neurotransmitter manufacture is disrupted, and serious behavioral problems can result.

The Role of Fat

We have already seen how the body breaks down its stores of fat into ketone bodies in times of glucose starvation. But what does the brain do with the fat we eat? Although a tiny amount is used for energy, the main job of fat in the brain is to maintain myelin. Myelin, we remember, is the substance around neurons and axons that conducts impulses quickly. Thus fat's contribution is very important.

Some of the glial cells produce myelin mainly from the fat and cholesterol in the diet. Fat is a part of all cell membranes, including those found in the brain. It can be classified into three groups—saturated, polyunsaturated, and monounsaturated. Saturated fat comes mainly from animal products, and along with cholesterol has been implicated in the development of arteriosclerosis, which leads to the blockage of arteries in the heart, brain, and rest of the body, and can eventually lead to heart attacks, strokes, and death. Polyunsaturated fats come mainly from vegetable fats and fish. These seem to provide protection against arterial blockage. Monounsaturated fats come from nuts, olives, and avocados. It too seems to protect the arteries.

25

Fat in our diet is broken down in the intestine into fatty acids and glycerol, which are absorbed and passed into circulation. The brain picks up these two breakdown products from the blood and uses them to form myelin.

All fatty acids except one can be made by the body from proteins and carbohydrates. The exception, a polyunsaturated fat called linoleic acid, is *the* essential dietary fatty acid— essential because the body cannot make it. Fortunately, it is extremely easy to find: one teaspoon of corn oil a day supplies an adult with all he or she needs. But that teaspoon is crucial for proper brain operation. Without it, the brain cannot repair its myelin sheaths, and the result may be a loss of coordination, confusion, memory loss, paranoia, apathy, tremors, and hallucinations. But don't worry if you haven't had any corn oil today—linoleic acid is found in almost all vegetable oils and many types of nuts (almonds, cashews, peanuts, walnuts, pecans).

Several cofactors (substances that aid in chemical reactions) are needed for this process. They include vitamins B_2 (riboflavin), B_3 (niacin), B_6 (pyridoxine), B_{12}, folacin, biotin, pantothenic acid, and copper—which brings us quite naturally to the next group of nutrients required for normal brain operation: vitamins and minerals.

The Need for Vitamins and Minerals

Almost all vitamins and minerals are needed by the brain in some manner for its proper growth, operation, maintenance, and repair. But some are more important than others.

In addition to amino acids, some vitamins and minerals are needed for the manufacture of neurotransmitters. These are: vitamin B_6 (found in meat, liver, whole grains, and fish); vitamin C (citrus fruits, potatoes, tomatoes, and green vegetables); and iron (red meats and dark green vegetables). To help in the chemical reactions that break down these nutrients for use by the brain, riboflavin (found in dairy products, organ meats, eggs, fish, green leafy vegetables) and folacin (liver, yeast, green leafy vegetables, meats) are needed.

Although glial cells produce myelin mainly from the cholesterol and fat in the diet, they also produce it by using vitamin B_{12}, and, this nutrient may be even more important in your diet than fat. Our bodies, as mentioned, can produce their own fat—from both carbohydrates and protein—but we cannot self-produce vitamin B_{12}. This vitamin is unique among nutrients—it is found almost exclusively in animal flesh and animal products. If you eat meat you get enough, and lacto-ovo vegetarians (those who eat eggs, milk, and cheese) are in good shape. But strict vegetarians, or vegans, must add vitamin B_{12} to their diets. Fortified soy milk is one good source, or a daily supplement of three mcg. of B_{12} in tablet form.

Without vitamin B_{12} we cannot maintain the myelin sheath surrounding the nerve fibers in adulthood, and even more critical, cannot promote their initial growth in childhood. A deficiency of B_{12} causes a creeping paralysis of the nerves and muscles, which begins at the extremities and works its way inward and up the spine. Once enough damage occurs to cause total paralysis, the condition cannot be reversed. Early symptoms include impaired vision, forgetfulness, confusion, bodily tremors, and paranoia. If caught, these conditions can be corrected.

Deficiencies of other vitamins and minerals principal to brain operation can cause equally serious symptoms. Vitamin B_1 is needed by the brain to obtain energy from glucose and protein, and it is involved in the neuronal conduction of messages. It is found in yeast, wheat germ, whole-grain cereals, nuts, beans, peas, green vegetables, milk, fish, poultry, and beef. Alcoholism and the abuse of antacids can cause and/or exacerbate a B_1 deficiency. Symptoms include memory loss, lack of general enthusiasm for life, and lack of coordination.

Vitamin B_6, found in meat, whole grains, and soy products, helps to make and break down neurotransmitters, and is also involved in myelin repair and the breakdown of protein. Smokers and women who take oral contraceptives are high risk for this B_6 deficiency, as are the elderly, heavy drinkers, teenagers, and pregnant and lactating women. Some symptoms are dry, itchy skin, particularly around the nose and mouth, dry and cracked lips, increased tiredness and depression (often just before a woman's period).

Iron is the component of many enzymes in the brain that are responsible for a variety of functions, ranging from breaking down nutrients in order to supply the brain with energy, to making neurotransmitters and the nucleic acid DNA. It is found in red meats and dark green vegetables like cabbage. Teenagers are in a high-risk group for iron deficiency, along with the elderly, premenopausal women, people who take a lot of aspirin, pregnant and lactating women, and vegetarians. Symptoms are weight gain, problems concentrating and remembering, headaches, and irritability.

These are the most important vitamins and minerals for a healthy brain. But all major vitamins and minerals play a role.

Balance, Balance, Balance!

To maintain overall physical and mental health, a well-balanced diet is always the first step. In fact, the key to understanding how to keep your body running like a well-oiled machine is the concept of balance. Nutrients and chemicals must be kept in balance relative to each other or problems will occur.

Illnesses or upsets create imbalances; imbalances aggravate illnesses. Too little vitamin B_6 in the diet can cause mental disturbances; eating too much saturated fat can lead to blockages in the arteries of the head and, as a result, impaired mental functioning. To stay healthy, we should maintain the delicate balance of chemicals in our brains through eating the proper foods. When upsets do occur, we should know how to correct these conditions by eating the specific nutrients needed to restore the brain's chemical balance.

Table 4

Nutrients Needed by the Adult Brain

THIAMINE (Vitamin B₁)

Function: Enables brain to get energy from glucose and protein; involved in nerve conduction of messages.

Daily Requirement: 1.5 mg.

Sources: Yeast, wheat germ, whole-grain cereals, nuts, beans, peas, green vegetables, milk, fish, poultry, organ meats, beef, pork. This vitamin is sensitive to alkaline cooking conditions (i.e., using baking soda).

Deficiencies: Anorexia, emotional instability, fatigue. Long-term deficiencies can result in degeneration of neurons and glial cells, resulting in a loss of recent memory, mental confusion, depression, apathy and a loss of some muscular coordination.

Stored in body: No.

High-Risk Groups: The elderly, heavy drinkers, heavy users of antacids and aspirin, children, lactating women.

RIBOFLAVIN (Vitamin B₂)

Function: Required for maintenance of myelin; makes energy available to brain from food substances; used in the breakdown of neurotransmitters; helps use nutrients for normal brain operation.

Daily Requirement: 1.7 mg.

Sources: Dairy products, liver and other organ meats, eggs, fish, green leafy vegetables, whole grains.

Deficiencies: Impaired brain growth in young children, behavioral abnormalities in adults.

Stored in body: No.

High-Risk Groups: The elderly, heavy drinkers, children, oral contraceptive users (especially if they are also athletes), lactating women, vegetarians.

NIACIN (Vitamin B₃)

Function: Helps brain obtain energy from glucose, fats, and protein; helps brain make myelin.

Daily Requirements: 19 mg.

Sources: Meats, nuts, cereals, beans, peas, yeast, fish, poultry.

Deficiencies: Depression, anxiety, hypersensitivity. fatigue, emotional instability, short-term memory problems, headaches. Long-term deficiencies lead to dementia, delirium, and nerve degeneration.

Stored in body: No.

High-Risk Groups: The elderly, children, lactating women.

Nutrients Needed by the Adult Brain

PYRIDOXINE (Vitamin B_6)
Function: Helps make and break down the neurotransmitters serotonin and GABA; involved in myelin repair; helps brain break down protein.
Daily Requirement: 2.3 mg.
Sources: Meat, liver, kidneys, whole grains, peanuts, soy products, fish, sweet potatoes.
Deficiencies: Can cause growth retardation in children and depression and/or hypersensitivity in adults. Although deficiencies are believed to be responsible for many of the symptoms of premenstrual syndrome [PMS], taking more than 250 mg. extra per day can be dangerous, as high doses of the vitamin have been shown to cause degeneration of the peripheral nerves. Long-term deficiencies cause abnormal electrical activity in the brain, which can lead to convulsions.
Stored in body: No.
High-Risk Groups: The elderly, heavy drinkers, oral contraceptive users, teenagers, children, smokers, pregnant and lactating women.

FOLIC ACID or FOLACIN
Function: Helps brain make proteins, fats, and DNA and RNA—the nucleic acids that play a key role in the manufacture of proteins in the body and the transmission of hereditary characteristics. Some of these proteins are enzymes—catalysts that speed up chemical reactions in the brain—and others are responsible for storing information. Folacin is also involved in the breakdown of neurotransmitters and the manufacture of acetylcholine (responsible for short-term memory).
Daily Requirement: 400 mcg.
Sources: Liver, yeast, green leafy vegetables, meats, poultry, fish, eggs, whole grains. Normal cooking temperatures cause a 65% loss of the vitamin.
Deficiencies: Growth retardation in infants. In adults, forgetfulness, apathy, irritability, insomnia, and depression. Prolonged deficiency leads to degeneration of peripheral nerves, psychosis, delirium, and dementia. A lack of folacin will lead to anemia and so will also cause oxygen deprivation of the brain, which may account for many of these symptoms.
Stored in Body: No.
High Risk Groups: The elderly, heavy drinkers, children, oral contraceptive users, teenagers, people taking a lot of aspirin, pregnant and lactating women.

Nutrients Needed by the Adult Brain

VITAMIN B$_{12}$
Function: Aids in manufacture of fat and protein, including the repair of myelin; keeps folic acid in its active, useful form.
Daily Requirement: 3 mcg.
Sources: Organ meats, fish, eggs, milk, cheese, poultry, muscle meats.
Deficiencies: Impaired myelin growth in infants and myelin degeneration in adults, resulting in loss of coordination, confusion, memory loss, paranoia, apathy. tremors, hallucinations. Anemia resulting from B$_{12}$ deficiency may be the cause of some of these symptoms as well, or at least contribute to them.
Stored in Body: Yes.
High-Risk Groups: The elderly, heavy drinkers, children, oral contraceptive users, smokers, vegetarians.

BIOTIN
Function: Helps brain make fat.
Daily Requirement: 300 mcg.
Sources: Liver, kidneys, yeast, beans, peas, chocolate, cauliflower, nuts, egg yolk.
Deficiencies: Rarely exist, but would lead to mild depression followed by extreme fatigue, muscle pain, and skin sensitivity.
Stored in Body: No.
High Risk Groups: None.

PANTOTHENIC ACID
Function: Helps brain use fats, carbohydrates, and proteins; helps it make fats, myelin, and acetylcholine.
Daily Requirement: 10 mg.
Sources: Beef, pork, chicken liver, wheat germ, peas, peanuts, yeast, fish, beans.
Deficiencies: Fatigue, anorexia, depression, insomnia, tingling in limbs' numbness, lack of coordination, and nausea. After long-term deficiency, degeneration of the nerves and myelin can occur.
Stored in body: No.
High Risk Groups: None.

Nutrients Needed by the Adult Brain

VITAMIN C
Function: Helps activate folacin; aids in iron absorption; helps brain use protein (including its use in neurotransmitter manufacture).

Daily Requirement: 60-100 mg.

Sources: Citrus fruits, potatoes, tomatoes, cantaloupe, cabbage, green vegetables, broccoli, peppers. C is easily degraded by exposure to the air. The C content of orange juice left in an open container decreases by as much as 30% in a 24-hour period.

Deficiencies: Hypersensitivity, depression, fatigue, weakness, headaches.

Stored in body: No.

High-Risk Groups: The elderly, children, oral contraceptive users, tee agers, smokers, people who take a lot of aspirin, lactating women.

VITAMIN A
Function: Protein and DNA manufacture.

Daily Requirement: 4000-5000 I.U.

Sources: All colored vegetables, fish, fish oil, liver, milk products, egg yolk, fortified margarine.

Deficiencies: Retarded brain growth and paralysis in infants; depression and apathy in adults due to degenerative changes in myelin and the structure of the neurons. Taking vitamin A in large doses is very dangerous. More than 25,000 units per day over an extended period of time, or a one-time dose of 300,000 units can lead to anorexia, irritability, fatigue, restlessness, headache, nausea, vomiting, and muscular weakness. Some deaths due to overdose have been reported.

Stored in body: Yes.

High-Risk Groups: The elderly, children, teenagers, people who frequently use laxatives.

Nutrients Needed by the Adult Brain

VITAMIN D
Function: Adequate absorption of calcium, which is used for normal neurotransmission.
Daily Requirement: 400 I.U.
Sources: Fortified milk, butter, margarine, eggs, liver, fish, cheese.
Deficiencies: Muscular twitching, spasms, and convulsions. Regular supplementation or one very high dose of several thousand units can be toxic, leading to irritability and anorexia.
Stored in Body: Yes.
High Risk Groups: The elderly, children, people who use laxatives frequently, pregnant and lactating women.

VITAMIN K
Function: Essential for the normal clotting of blood.
Daily Requirement: 100-300 mcg.
Sources: Asparagus, bacon, bread, broccoli, cabbage, cheese, lettuce, liver, oats, spinach, turnip greens, watercress. It is also made in the intestine by bacteria.
Deficiencies: A tendency for the brain to bleed.
Stored in body: Yes.
High Risk Groups: The elderly and people taking drugs that prevent the blood from clotting.

IRON
Function: Responsible for many functions, ranging from breaking down nutrients in order to supply brain energy, to making neurotransmitters and DNA.
Daily Requirement: 18 mg.
Sources: Red meat and dark green vegetables like cabbage. You absorb about 30% of the iron from meats, and about 10% from vegetables.
Deficiencies: Anemia, robbing the brain of oxygen and energy. Children become irritable, anorexic, inattentive, and hyperactive with the associated learning problems; adults have problems concentrating, are irritable, and have frequent headaches. Excess iron intake is toxic and can impair general brain operation.
High-Risk Groups: The elderly, premenopausal women, teenagers, people taking a lot of aspirin, pregnant and lactating women, vegetarians.

Nutrients Needed by the Adult Brain

ZINC
Function: Involved in brain reactions that liberate energy from glucose and protein; helps make RNA, DNA and protein.

Daily Requirement: 15 mg.

Sources: Meat, liver, eggs, seafood, milk, whole grains. Zinc is not absorbed well from its vegetable sources.

Deficiencies: Impaired brain growth in children; deficient adults and children develop anorexia, mental lethargy, and irritability. Too much zinc is toxic, and this can also occur when acidic foods or drinks have been allowed to stand for long periods of time in galvanized containers (which many contain toxic levels of this trace mineral). Toxicity causes nausea, exhaustion, dizziness, and drowsiness.

Stored in Body: Yes.

High-Risk Groups: The elderly, heavy drinkers, children, oral contraceptive users, teenagers, pregnant and lactating women, vegetarians.

COPPER
Function: Brain's production of energy from nutrients and for formation/maintenance of myelin.

Daily Requirement: 2-3 mg.

Sources: Nuts, shellfish, liver, peas, raisins, beans, dried fruits, fresh fruit.

Deficiencies: Anemia leading to depression in adults, and brain growth retardation in children.

Stored in body: Yes.

High-Risk Groups: Infants (seven to nine months of age), people, who take zinc supplements.

MANGANESE
Function: Helps brain make fats and myelin, as well as protein; helps brain extract energy from nutrients.

Daily Requirement: 2.5-5 mg.

Sources: Wheat, cereals, grains, nuts, leafy vegetables, meat.

Deficiencies: No visible or reported symptoms.

High-Risk Groups: None.

Nutrients Needed by the Adult Brain

MAGNESIUM

Function: Helps brain get energy from nutrients.

Daily Requirement: 300-350 mg.

Sources: Cereals, dark green vegetables, nuts, beans, peas, seafood, chocolate, cocoa.

Deficiencies: Depression, lethargy, confusion; in severe cases, seizures.

High-Risk Groups: Heavy drinkers, oral contraceptive users, people who take diuretics.

CALCIUM

Function: Regulates activity of neurons, enabling them to send messages: activates enzymes that make energy available to the brain.

Daily Requirement: 1,000 mg.

Sources: Dairy products, vegetables, cereals, beans, peas. Calcium is most readily absorbed from dairy products—only 10% of the calcium found in vegetables is absorbed.

Deficiencies: Muscular spasms, due to over-susceptibility of the nerve cells to stimuli (this happens only in extreme, prolonged cases).

Stored in body: Yes.

High-Risk Groups: The elderly, teenagers, people who frequently use laxatives or antacids containing aluminum, smokers, pregnant and lactating women, vegetarians, people who take diuretics.

SODIUM

Function: Essential for normal neurotransmission.

Daily Requirement: 1.1-3.3 grams.

Sources: Most food substances, excluding fresh fruit and vegetables.

Deficiencies: Loss of appetite, nausea, vomiting, impaired senses.

Stored in Body: Yes:

High-Risk Groups: People taking certain diuretics, such as thiazides, spironolactone, and captopril, those taking drugs which cause water retention such as those used to reduce blood glucose levels (chlorpropamide, tolbutamide).

Nutrients Needed by the Adult Brain

POTASSIUM
Function: Essential for normal neurotransmission.
Daily Requirement: 1.9-5.6 grams.
Sources: Bananas. orange juice, potatoes, tomatoes, pumpkins, artichokes, winter squash, apricots, avocados, honeydew melon, nectarines, peaches, prunes, raisins, peanuts, walnuts, milk, meat.
Deficiencies: Weakness, loss of appetite, nausea, vomiting, listlessness, apprehension. Drowsiness, stupor and irrationality can develop in extreme cases.
Stored in Body: Yes.
High-Risk Groups: People taking certain diuretics, such as thiazides, furosemide, and ethacrynic acid; people using certain laxatives, such as phenolphthalein, bisacodyl, and senna. Also, those who use aspirin in large doses, take corticosteroids, antibiotics (gentamicin, amphotericin B), or take levodopa.

IODINE
Function: Essential for normal brain growth and development.
Daily Requirement: 150-200 mcg.
Sources: Baked goods, cheese, eggs, kelp, meat, milk, iodized salt, seafood and vegetables.
Deficiencies: Mental retardation in the growing infant.
Stored in Body: Yes.
High-Risk Groups: People living at high altitudes remote from the sea who do not use iodized salt.

PHOSPHORUS
Function: Essential for the release of energy from food substances and for the formation of enzymes and cells.
Daily Requirement: 1,000 mg.
Sources: Nuts, apricots, bran, cereals, cheese, fish, liver, milk and peas.
Deficiencies: Confusion.
Stored in Body: Yes.
High-Risk Groups: Elderly and people taking large amounts of antacids.

Nutrients Needed by the Adult Brain

GLUCOSE
Function: Provides energy for the brain. Drives the sodium pump, helps build new tissues.
Daily Requirement: 110 grams.
Sources: Starches, vegetables, fruits, sugars. milk.
Deficiencies: Dizziness, fatigue, fainting, confusion, coma, brain damage. A gradual switch to ketone bodies for energy use during a prolonged fast can lead to the breakdown of vital tissue, such as that of the heart muscle.
Stored in body: In limited amounts.
High-Risk Groups: Diabetics, hypoglycemics.

PROTEIN
Function: Builds new cells; repairs myelin sheaths; manufactures neurotransmitters, enzymes, and hormones.
Daily Requirement: 45 grams from animal sources, or 65 grams from vegetable sources.
Sources: Meat, fish, beans, peas, lentils, soy products, dairy products, eggs.
Deficiencies: In prolonged and extreme cases, a wide variety of mental and behavioral disturbances.
Stored in body: Yes.
High-Risk Groups: Vegetarians.

FAT
Function: Maintains myelin; is part of all cell membranes. Body fat is broken down into ketone bodies and used for energy in times of glucose shortage.
Daily Requirement: 20-25% of total daily calories.
Sources: Vegetable oils, vegetables, meat, fish, dairy products, nuts.
Deficiencies: Deficiencies in linoleic acid can cause loss of coordination, confusion, memory loss, paranoia, apathy, tremors, and hallucinations.
Stored in body: Yes, except for linoleic acid.
High-Risk Groups: People with chronic diarrhea.

PART TWO

Correcting Problems Through Diet

CHAPTER 3

FIGHTING STRESS

Stress is a word we use today with almost casual regularity. Most of us assume that stress is a part of living and cannot be avoided. This is true to some extent, but there are ways we can offset damaging physical reactions to stressful situations. Ten people may attend a highly emotional and stressful business meeting; five may suffer mildly from it, four may suffer heavily, and one may take it in his stride. It's not the stress that's the problem—it's the way your body reacts to it. And your body's reactions are decided by the brain.

The word stress covers a wide variety of conditions. Any type of change in the environment—positive or negative—can cause the body stress. This includes exposure to extreme heat or cold; pain; illness; injury; accident; exposure to toxic compounds, radiation, pollution, and other environmental irritants; excessive excitement; or a surprise. A gall-bladder operation can impose tremendous stress on the body as can a vacation.

To the body, the cause is irrelevant; it reacts to all stress in the same way. The only thing that changes is the degree of the reaction, and that is determined by the amount of stress. The body responds to stress with something called the "fight-or-flight" response, which makes you ready to deal effectively with any possible danger. This reaction can also stimulate you in positive ways, by helping you solve problems and overcome great obstacles. On the other hand, it can destroy your health.

The fight-or-flight, or stress response is designed to help the body cope with physical danger. The catch here is that most of the stressful "danger" encountered these days is more emotional in nature. The response makes the body ready for vigorous muscular activity, not for the anxiety-ridden state suffered by a person trying to hide the stress-related problems to which he is unable to respond actively.

The reaction begins when your brain perceives a threat to your stability, which can be as slight as a loud noise near your ear. What follows is a chain of physical events, acting through both the nerves and hormones, which causes a state of readiness to develop in every part of your body. The chain starts when the alarm signal causes an emotion like fear or anger to appear in the brain. This causes the hypothalamus to secrete a substance called *corticotrophin releasing factor* (CRF), which it sends to the pituitary gland. The pituitary responds in turn by secreting *adrenocorticotrophic hormone* (ACTH) into the bloodstream. Moments later, this hormone reaches the adrenal glands and causes them to release the neurotransmitters epinephrine and norepinephrine; enkephalins, which are short chains of amino acids that suppress pain; and steroids, which speed up metabolism.

The amount of epinephrine found in the blood stream during this type of reaction is up to 300 times the normal amount. Epinephrine interacts with the cells in various organs, increasing the heart rate and blood pressure, and causing the release of extra sugar from the liver for the purpose of providing energy to the brain and muscles. At the same time, blood vessels supplying the skin and digestive system contract, slowing down the digestive rate and drawing color from the skin. In this situation, if you cut yourself, the blood would clot more rapidly than usual. The chest expands as the breath comes faster and deeper in order to supply more oxygen to the brain and muscles, since glucose and other fuels must be combined with oxygen to yield energy. The pupils of the eyes dilate so that you can see better; the muscles tense so that you can jump, run, or fight with top speed and strength; the mouth becomes dry as saliva output falls; the body sweats in readiness to cool itself during violent activity. In extreme cases of fear, the bladder or rectum may empty, and the hair really can stand on end.

These effects are reinforced by messages sent down the nerves from the hypothalamus to the organs and glands affected by the stress response. This all-out reaction provides excellent support when you need to take any type of emergency physical action. And anyone can respond in this highly efficient way to stress of a sudden physical nature for a short period of time. But if the stress is prolonged, and especially if a physical action is not a permitted response to it, it can drain your body of its reserves and leave it weakened, aged, and more susceptible to illness.

Body Reserves Used During Times of Stress

During stress, increased supplies may be needed of all three energy fuels—carbohydrate, fat, and protein. If the response required is heavy physical action, and involves injury, all three are used. Because in such a situation the body is too occupied with responding to eat, internal sources are drained for these fuels.

Conserving body water at this time is essential, and the body has several ways of doing this. First, it retains sodium. But to do so the kidneys exchange, and lose, potassium. This is why your body needs sufficient stores of potassium. Sodium retention can also lead to high blood pressure. In addition, the raised levels of norepinephrine during stress also tend to raise blood pressure. A combination of the two over an extended period of time can result in permanent elevations in blood pressure and result in an increased risk of heart attack or stroke.

For energy, glucose is taken from stored glycogen in the liver and muscles. The supply is exhausted within one day. After that, body protein provides the only continuing glucose supply, and this is mainly drawn from the muscles. Some tissues can use fat for energy, and if you regularly eat balanced meals, your fat stores are sufficient to meet this need for several days. In other words, the body uses not only dispensible supplies—those which are there to be used up, like fat—but also functional tissue that you don't want to lose, like muscle.

So in preparation for long periods of stress (such as an extended illness), you want to have as much protein in the muscle tissue as possible. You also need to make sure that you minimize the wasting of muscle.

Another nutrient lost from the body during stress is calcium, which is taken from the bones. People lose varying amounts of this essential bone mineral, depending partly on their hormonal state (although studies do not yet totally confirm this). Adult bone loss is common anyway, and so the same measures

TABLE 5

Good Food Sources of Protein
(Each portion provides approximately 20 g of protein)

FOOD	AMOUNT (ounces)
baked beans	1 1/2
beef, cooked, lean or fat	3
beef, ground, cooked	3
beef, sirloin steak, cooked, lean or fat	3
calf's liver, fried	3
cheese, blue	3
cheese, Cheddar	3
cheese, cottage	2/3 cup
chicken, cooked	2
eggs,	3
lamb chop, cooked	3
lentils, cooked	1 1/4 cups
milk, full-cream or skimmed	2 1/2 cups
pork, loin, cooked	3
peanuts, roasted	3
salmon, cooked	3
shrimp, cooked	3
sunflower seeds	3
tuna, tinned in oil, drained	3
veal cutlet, cooked	3
yogurt, low fat, fruit-flavored	16

should be taken here as with protein—increase your body's reserves.

Preparing the Body For Stress

A healthy body, with tissues that contain the best possible amounts of all essential nutrients, is well-prepared to take on stress. The type of balanced diet that will produce such a body must include a daily intake of the following:

- 2-3 servings of vegetables (raw and cooked)
- 2-3 servings of fruits (raw and cooked)
- 3-4 servings of whole-grain products
- 1-2 servings of poultry, meat, fish, eggs, beans, or peas

(See what is meant as a serving size in the tables that follow)

As mentioned, protein and calcium are two of the vital nutrients needed to cope with stress, and so you must get ample supplies of both of them into your body.

However, it is not enough to eat foods that contain protein and calcium. You must exercise to enable the body to use them effectively. Muscles cannot grow and retain protein without activity. They don't respond passively to the environment, but actively, to the demands placed on them. Only when they have to work do they develop and accumulate protein. To be in the best of health, then, you must pay attention to both diet *and* exercise. Plan daily or every-other-day workouts that are demanding enough to build up muscle tissue. This can be done easily, by starting with only 20 minutes of vigorous exercise every other day. In this way, when you encounter a stressful situation, even if eating is cut down or out for a short time, the wasting of muscles will be less severe. Also, if you increase your muscle mass, you will add significantly to your body's supply of potassium.

Bones, too, need active work to build up their calcium stores. In response to the "good stress" of physical work, your bones store calcium and become denser, stronger, and able to carry more weight. Like the muscles, when they are confronted with the "bad stress" of anxiety or illness, they can better afford to give up some of their calcium stores without becoming weak. So, to prepare for stress eat a balanced diet and exercise regularly. This will minimize any damage to the body during trying times.

Nutrition During Stress

You usually find you have less of an appetite during stressful times. This is an adaptive reaction to a physical threat. The brain knows that energy is needed to carry out the fight-or-flight response rather than to look for or eat food. The blood supply has been redirected to the muscles in order to maximize strength and speed and so even if you do eat, you may not be able to digest or absorb the food efficiently. In fact, during time of extreme upset, the stomach and intestines may even reject solid food, causing you to vomit or suffer from

---

TABLE 6

Good Food Sources of Calcium
(Each portion provides approximately 500 mg. of calcium)

FOOD	AMOUNT
Almonds	1 cup
Amaranth	4 oz.
Broccoli	2 1/4 cups
Cheese:	
cottage	12 oz.
sandwich-type	1 1/2 to 2 oz.
Custard	1 cup
Fish (canned):*	
mackerel	3 1/2 oz.
salmon	5 1/2 oz.
sardines	3 1/2 oz.
Ice Cream	1 2/3 cups
Kelp	1 1/2 oz.
Milk:	
whole, low-fat, or buttermilk	8 oz.
Tofu (soybean curd)	8 oz.
Tortillas (6 in. diam.)	5
Brewers yeast	14 tablespoons
Yogurt	3/4-4/5 cup

*This calcium level includes the softened bones. If the bones are discarded, the calcium content will be greatly reduced.
(If dairy products are not high on your list of priorities take a 1,000 mg. supplement of calcium as calcium carbonate which means taking two and a half grams.)

---

diarrhea. This all means that when you are undergoing severe stress you shouldn't force yourself to eat, as it may not serve any useful purpose anyway.

On the other hand, fasting is not a good idea either, and the longer one fasts, the harder it is to start eating normally again. A vicious cycle can develop from prolonged fasting; the person under severe stress cannot eat, and by not eating becomes less able to handle the stress. The problem can be complicated by the fact that most people exposed to stress secrete extra acid in their stomachs which, without eating, can lead to ulcers. It is best not to let stress become so all-consuming that eating stops. Managing stress so that it does not overwhelm you is both a nutritional and psychological task.

If you are under stress and *can* eat, you should definitely do so. If you can eat only a small amount of food, then it is best to

TABLE 7

Good Food Sources of Potassium

FOOD	SERVING SIZE	POTASSIUM (mg)
Apricots, dried	1 cup	1,273
Avocado, Florida	1	1,836
Banana	1 small	440
Beans, lima	1 cup	724
Brussels sprouts, fresh cooked	1 cup	423
Carrots, cooked	1 cup	344
Chicken, broiled	6 ounces	483
Clams, soft	3 ounces	225
Dates, pitted	10	518
Flounder	6 ounces	1,000
Milk, skim	1 cup	406
Orange juice	1 cup	496
Potato, baked	1 medium	782
Prunes, dried and pitted	5 large	298
Spinach, chopped and cooked	1 cup	688
Sweetbreads	3 ounces	433
Tomato, raw	1 medium	300
Tuna, salt-free, canned	1 small container	327
Yogurt, plain	1 container	531

eat a little bit many times during the day. Drink plenty of fluids, especially water, along with the food.

Whenever a person under stress stops eating, nutrients are of course depleted. In addition to protein and calcium, potassium levels are affected. You need at least 2,000 mg. of potassium per day during stressful times.

The other nutrients most likely to be depleted are the vitamins and minerals that the body does not store in adequate quantities. Water-soluble vitamins like C and the B vitamins are especially at risk during stress when the body has a higher requirement for them. The adrenal glands, which are working particularly hard, have the highest concentration of vitamin C of all the tissues in the body, and the brain has the second highest. C is crucial to the production of the neurotransmitters norepinephrine and epinephrine. If you make sure to get 100 mg. a day of vitamin C into your diet you will have enough to offset the losses produced by stress.

The boosted metabolic rate and the increased manufacture of neurotransmitters will step up your need for the B-complex vitamins—but not enough to cause a deficiency as long as you get the RDA for these vitamins into your diet.* However if you are not eating properly during stressful times (especially when prolonged) it is best to take a daily vitamin-mineral supplement that supplies a balanced assortment of all necessary nutrients. This supplement should not contain "megadoses" of these nutrients, but amounts close to the RDA. In general, if you are eating fewer than 1,200 to 1,500 calories a day you need this supplement.

New evidence from experiments done on animals has provided us with additional information on how to cope with stress. It was shown that the brain is unable to produce normal levels of norepinephrine when subject to extreme stress. As a result, the brain cannot signal the body to cope with the stress efficiently. However, if the animals studied were given a high-tyrosine diet, the brain levels of norepinephrine were perfectly suited to cope with the stress. (Norepinephrine, as you recall, is made from the amino acid tyrosine.) This research

---

*B_1 = 1.5 mg.; B_2 = 1.7 mg.; B_3 = 20 mg.; B_6 = 2-3 mg.

raises the issue of whether tyrosine supplements might be beneficial for humans exposed to severe stress. It takes 25-50 milligrams of tyrosine per pound of body weight (110 lb. person = 2.5 grams) spaced out during the day to maintain brain tyrosine levels in humans above the norm.

Eating Too Much?

Although some people can't eat during stressful times, others eat too much. Some people overeat because the actual act relieves the stress by occupying the nervous system with a familiar activity. In addition, eating, or the food eaten, causes the release of soothing substances, like specific neurotransmitters, in the brain.

Certain types of stress cause the production of morphine-like substances in the brain (i.e., endorphins) which promote eating. Some proteins, when they are digested, also apparently release *peptides*, which have a sedating effect. More research needs to be done in this area, but for now let us say that people who for whatever reason overeat when confronted with stress can become obese. Therefore, they should find some other form of behavior to release the tension—such as exercise, meditation, or a hobby.

Overeating during stress again points out the necessity for exercise. In the stress response, muscle fuels, including fats and sugar, flood the bloodstream. If you are very active, this excess fat will be burned up. But if you stay stuck to your office chair, the fat is more likely to collect in your blood vessels and clog up your arteries. Exercise (even if it is punching pillows) helps to relieve tension, and also may release pain-killing chemicals in the nervous system that can alleviate to some degree a dark mood, or ease physical pain and illness.

Nutrition after Recovery

When a period of great stress is over and the body can recover, you should replenish your depleted body stores. If you have lost weight, gain it back through healthy eating and exercise, to replenish both lean and fat tissue. If you have gained weight, diet and exercise to remove the unwanted pounds. You should also learn how to better prepare yourself both nutritionally and emotionally for the next stressful situation that comes your way.

Who Is Most Susceptible to Stress?

Everyone experiences stress. The situation can be as simple as sitting in a hot car during rush-hour traffic. But short-term stress is rarely a problem. Your body has what it needs to deal with a bad day. It is the long-term kind, caused by situations like a bad marriage or a high-pressure job, that can cause heart trouble, stroke, or numerous other diseases.

Research shows that the following are the most 20 most stressful situations a person can encounter, with respect to their effects on the body and brain (note that they are not all bad situations):

- death of spouse
- divorce
- marital separation
- jail term
- death of close family member
- injury or illness
- marriage
- being fired from the job
- marital reconciliation
- retirement
- change in health status of family member
- pregnancy
- sexual difficulties
- gain of new family member
- business adjustment
- change in financial status (up or down)
- death of a close friend
- change in occupation
- change in number of arguments with spouse
- mortgage, or debts over $10,000

Different people have different reactions to stress, and so may suffer from different types of illnesses. For instance, many heart patients exhibit what is called Type A personality—making them overanxious, overtense overachievers. The people who are most susceptible to adverse physical reactions from stress are: those who have what is popularly (and to a degree erroneously) called an "artistic temperament"—they are passionate about everything they do, and may experience tremendous swings in mood, from extreme highs to despairing lows; those who find doing anything a real trial, and react at a slow pace. Obese people, as well as those who are lethargic or depressed, fall into this category.

Even-tempered people who work hard and play hard are the least susceptible. But someone who seems calm all the time may not really fit this bill. Some quiet people are actually hiding their feelings, and are boiling under the surface with repressions or frustrations. These closet sufferers are actually at risk for the greatest stress reactions.

Stress and Disease

Stress also impairs the operation of the body's immune system. The multitude of chemicals released during the stress response can bind to the white blood cells and make them less efficient in killing bacteria. We have already seen how stress can cause ulcers, hypertension, and heart disease. Prolonged stress may even increase the risk of getting cancer. However, it is important to remember that it is not the stress itself that causes disease, but your reaction to it.

How to Avoid Stress

Some simple stress-management techniques should be mentioned here as a form of preventive medicine:

- Eat a balanced diet.
- Exercise.
- Change the way you see stressful events—view them as challenges you can deal with, rather than fearful events you would like to run away from.
- Take time out to relax and enjoy yourself. Learn relaxation techniques, or find a hobby.
- Express yourself as openly as possible, rather than holding many of your most extreme emotions inside.
- Use friends to help you through times of stress. A good support system eases some of the emotional burden.
- Don't let yourself get too upset over minor irritants, like slow-moving lines in the supermarket.

• Maintain a proper perspective on the situation. Ask yourself, "Will this matter to me a year from now?"

How to Cope

During a prolonged stressful situation, make sure you get enough:

- protein: 45 g for women, 55 g for men
- calcium: 1,000 mg.
- potassium: 2,000-5,000 mg.
- vitamin C: 100 mg.
- vitamin B_1: 1.5 mg.
- vitamin B_2: 1.7 mg.
- vitamin B_3: 20 mg.
- vitamin B_6: 2-3 mg.
- tyrosine: 25-50 mg. per pound of body weight

CHAPTER 4

REGULATING YOUR MOODS

Although some people boast that they have total control over their emotions, that is not the case with most of us. It is easy to see how sudden mood or emotional changes can disrupt our daily lives. A businessperson suddenly feels depressed and bored by his or her job and loses the motivation needed to function. A mother, exhausted after the day's chores, finds it harder to get a good night's sleep and so her exhaustion escalates. A college student becomes so riddled with anxiety over an exam in a difficult course that he or she can't seem to comprehend the material.

Most of us find ourselves beset by periods of "highs" and "lows," which often seem to come out of the blue. In milder cases, we often ignore these slight mood changes, but in severe instances a sudden emotional change can cause true upheaval and lead to serious behavioral problems. Stress increases, depression threatens to descend, and a good night's sleep becomes an elusive dream.

Whether or not we are severely affected by mood changes, we would all like to have a greater degree of control over our emotional natures. To shake off depression when it strikes, to pull oneself out of lethargy and get back to work, to get a sound night's sleep—these are all abilities we crave. And all these things can often be obtained by a specific type of diet that manipulates the levels of mood-controlling neurotransmitters in the brain.

Neurotransmitters have a profound effect on the way you feel, and the specific behavior patterns you exhibit in everyday life. They also affect your physical health: directly, through physical changes, and indirectly, through mood changes. People who have little control over their moods appear to suffer from more diseases of all types. So, controlling your emotional nature has a physical side effect.

In some cases, extreme imbalances in neurotransmitter levels can lead to severe mental or physical illnesses. For example, an excess of dopamine in the brain has now been linked to schizophrenia; a deficiency of dopamine leads to Parkinson's disease.

For less severe problems—depression, pain, insomnia—dietary changes and/or supplements can often make a big difference, and emotional control can then become an easily achievable goal instead of an impossible dream.

Depression

There exists two popularly held explanations for the onset of depression. One theory attributes it to a low level of brain serotonin, the other to a low level of brain norepinephrine. Almost all of the drugs psychiatrists use to treat depression increase the levels of one or both of these neurotransmitters. But if you don't want to reach for a pill, changing your diet can often help just as much. You can raise your brain's level of norepinephrine by getting more tyrosine into your diet, along with the amino acid phenylalanine (which can be made into tyrosine in the brain), since tyrosine makes norepinephrine. The same is true of tryptophan, which makes serotonin, and so can raise these brain levels when you get enough of it into your body.

Both tyrosine and tryptophan (which are marketed in stores with an "L" in front of their names) have been shown to be useful in the treatment of unipolar depression, a condition that causes mood swings from a normal and well-adjusted to withdrawal, sadness, and lethargy. (These substances are, however, of no value in treating bipolar depression, in which mood swings range from irrational elation to total depression.)

Tryptophan and Depression

Tryptophan is most useful in treating depression when the person also has a craving for carbohydrates. It is believed that such cravings reflect inadequate brain serotonin levels—that is, the brain is asking for more carbohydrates in order to increase its serotonin levels.

When you consume a carbohydrate—rich, low-protein meal, this reduces the blood levels of most amino acids—but not tryptophan. Thus there is more room for tryptophan on the transport mechanism that gives entry into the brain. After eating a high-carbohydrate meal, brain levels of tryptophan rise, and this increases brain serotonin levels.

Although the increases produced by eating a high-carbohydrate meal are small, taking a tryptophan supplement greatly increases relative brain levels. Protein-rich meals have, of course, the opposite effect, decreasing both tryptophan and serotonin levels.

If you are suffering from depression and also find yourself craving carbohydrates, try changing to a carbohydrate-rich diet. No more than 10-15% of your total calories should come from protein sources and 55-60% from carbohydrates. (Tables 8 and 9 list foods rich in carbohydrate and protein, respectively.) If this doesn't seem to have much of an effect, a daily supplement of one to three grams of tryptophan might be the answer. It should be taken in three equal doses (for example, three does of 800 mg) after meals. The effects of tryptophan last for only a few hours, which is why repeated doses are necessary. Taking the supplement after meals will prevent the nausea some people experience as a side effect. (Obviously, the lower the dose the better; experiment within the dosage range in order to see at which level you get concrete results.)

Many obese people suffer from this type of depression, as do many women with premenstrual syndrome (PMS). Another interesting group are those who suffer from "seasonal depression." In these people, the symptoms appear each year during seasons of decreasing daylight. The yearning for carbohydrates increases during the fall and winter, when their depression is at its worst, and eases up, along with the depression, in spring and summer. We are not yet sure why this happens.

Tyrosine and Depression

Tyrosine (along with phenylalanine) and tryptophan share the same carrier mechanism for entry into the brain. This means that you can increase your levels of tryptophan *or* tyrosine. In fact, increasing one decreases the other. A meal rich in carbohydrates reduces the amount of norepinephrine made in the brain from tyrosine. A protein-rich meal, on the other hand, elevates these levels. The changes produced by a high-protein diet alone are small, but tryosine supplements can have dramatic effects. Initial tests using tyrosine to treat depressed patients have been encouraging: one to three grams of tyrosine taken daily at spaced intervals are often the answer.

TABLE 8

Good Food Sources of Carbohydrates*

All carbohydrate-rich foods have the same effect of elevating brain serotonin levels, irrespective of their degrees of sweetness.

Simple	Complex
Cake	Beans
Candy	Bread
Cookies	Carrots
Corn syrup	Cereal
Fruit, dried	Corn
Fruit, fresh	Crackers
Honey	Nuts
Jam	Parsnips
Jelly	Pasta
Molasses	Peas
Soft Drinks	Potatoes
Sugar, maple	Sweet potatoes
Sugar, table	Winter squash

*A simple carbohydrate has no food value apart from its energy content. But complex carbohydrates are rich in nutrients and are essential to your body.

Taking the tyrosine with meals avoids mild stomach upsets (due to tryosine's acidity). Never take more than three grams without the supervision of your doctor.

Obviously, we are advising two very different treatments regarding depression. The tryptophan route appears to work in people with depression coupled with carbohydrate cravings. Tyrosine works on depression in people without carbohydrate cravings, and can be effective in the treatment of lethargy (the lack of interest in doing anything) in people over the age of 40. If there is no clear-cut way of determining which route to take, experimenting for a short period of time with one method and then the other, will clearly show the way.

TABLE 9

Good Food Sources of Protein

(Each portion provides approximately 20g of protein)

FOOD	AMOUNT (Ounces)
baked beans	1 1/2
beef, cooked, lean or fat	3
beef, ground, cooked	3
beef, sirloin steak, cooked, lean or fat	3
calf's liver, fried	3
cheese, blue	3
cheese, Cheddar	3
cheese, cottage	2/3 cup
chicken, cooked	2
eggs, 3	
lamp chop, cooked	3
lentils, cooked	1 1/4 cups
milk, full-cream or skimmed	2 1/2 cups
pork, loin, cooked	3
peanuts, roasted	3
salmon, cooked	3
shrimp, cooked	3
sunflower seeds	3
tuna, tinned in oil, drained	3
veal cutlet, cooked	3
yogurt, low fat, fruit-flavored	16

Diet Versus Drugs

Many people feel that controlling depression through natural, dietary supplements and adjustments is preferable to the use of antidepressant drugs, like MAO inhibitors or tricyclic antidepressants. Pharmaceutical cures are often like hitting a walnut with a sledge-hammer—they're just too strong for the need, and can cause other imbalances in the body that then also have to be corrected. Unlike pharmaceuticals, your body does not develop a tolerance to either tryptophan or tryosine, since they are normal components of your body's biochemical structure. Therefore, there will be no need to take more and more of the supplement to achieve the same effect (although this is not necessarily a problem with antidepressant drugs, either).

However in cases of massive, ongoing depression, or true emotional imbalances that severely disrupt a person's life, a doctor's care and strong medication are advised. These simple dietary supplements are intended for people who are usually well balanced, suffering only rarely or occasionally from depression and/or lethargy. The emotionally ill, on the other hand, show dramatic changes in neurotransmitter levels, and these cannot be corrected by dietary supplements.

How Do You Sleep?

There is nothing more frustrating than the inability to fall asleep naturally, even when the body is exhausted. The brain needs sleep and cannot function very well without it, especially if sleeplessness is prolonged. As many as 15% of all patients seeking help from their doctors complain of some form of insomnia. These bouts of sleeplessness usually do not last for long and don't affect your overall longevity—but they can interfere with daily functioning and cause irritability and physical pains.

A great number of studies done over the past 20 years have shown that tryptophan helps many people fall asleep. It benefits most those who have mild insomnia, or take a longer time than average to fall asleep (more than 10-30 minutes). Tryptophan won't help you if you suffer from severe insomnia or anxiety-related insomnia. Nonetheless, a recent report showed that 30% of older people suffering from sleeplessness benefited from the administration of tryptophan.

One gram of tryptophan should be taken with a carbohydrate-rich snack containing less than 10% of its calories as protein (such as a few cookies, a slice of cake, a muffin, a granola bar, or chocolate) about 45 to 60 minutes before you go to bed. Actually, it's the cookies in the old "milk and cookies before bed" combination that the body needs to sleep easily and soundly, *not* the protein-rich milk. Milk is a source of tryptophan, but not a good enough source to compensate for the competing neutral amino acids it contains.

If this works for you, you will begin to feel sleepy in 45-90 minutes. You will fall asleep more easily and faster, wake up fewer times during the night, and sleep for a longer period of time. People over the age of 40 may need up to three grams to get this full effect.

Tryptophan helps people sleep in one of two ways (researchers are not yet sure which one it is). It either works by raising brain serotonin levels, or by lowering the amount of tyrosine getting into the brain. Dopamine, like norepinephrine, is made from tyrosine in the brain and is believed to aid in keeping you awake. Neurotransmitters, as we have seen, operate by nature of their relative levels and so a predominance of serotonin over dopamine in the sleep center at the base of the brain could be the cause of the helpful effect tryptophan doses produce.

There are two major categories of sleep—deep or quiet, regular sleep; and REM (rapid eyeball movement) sleep. During deep sleep, a person lies very still, breathes evenly and regularly, and the eyes stay at rest. It is during this time that people are hardest to awaken and can sleep walk. In an adult, over 80% of sleep time is spent in this state. The REM sleep period is marked by lighter sleep, restlessness, irregular breathing and, naturally, rapid eye movement. During this time, about 75% of your dreams take place, and they tend to be more vivid, sexual, and bizarre than in deep sleep. Nightmares normally occur during the REM period.

Taking tryptophan at the dosage levels we recommend does not alter the percentage of sleeping time spent in either of the two categories, and it doesn't change the quality of sleep at any time. But people taking sleep medications (benzodiazepines or barbiturates) tend to spend less time in REM sleep and their quality of sleep is altered—it becomes less restful to the body and mind. This tends to make the users of such drugs drowsy the next morning and less able to concentrate, whereas tryptophan users feel better rested and more attentive than they did during their sleepless days. With chronic use of sleeping pills the body builds up resistance to the drugs and needs increased doses, often to a dangerous level. Also, when a person stops taking these types of pills he or she can suffer from worse insomnia than before. None of this happens with tryptophan therapy. However, unlike tryptophan, the benzodiazepines (i.e., Valium, Librium) reduce anxiety levels in normal as well as in anxious people and so are better for treating anxiety-induced insomnia.

• Cut out caffeine-containing foods and beverages in the evening hours. Consuming them results in lighter sleep and more frequent periods of awakening during the night.

• Omit alcohol as much as possible. Although it may help you fall asleep initially, it will not keep you asleep. Once the alcohol wears off, you may wake up and not be able to get back to sleep. The type of sleep alcohol induces is also not a natural one, and does not thoroughly rest the body and mind.

• Do not eat dinner so early that you are hungry right before bedtime.

Tryptophan—A Way out of Pain?

Chronic pain can disrupt every aspect of a person's life. Over $60 billion a year are spent in diagnosing and treating chronic pain, not to mention the lost earnings experienced by the sufferers. Over the last few years, studies have shown that tryptophan-enriched diets increase the pain-killing effects of endorphins (the body's natural pain-killers) and increase a person's tolerance to chronic pain. For maximum benefit, 500 mg. of tryptophan should be taken six times a day (every three hours) and a high-carbohydrate diet should be followed.

When considering tryptophan as an alternative to regular analgesics like aspirin, remember that no matter when tryptophan is taken, it tends to cause drowsiness, lethargy, and lapses in concentration in some people. However, it does not impair coordination or mental abilities. In other words, your driving skill will not be altered, but you may find it more difficult staying alert at the wheel. In the same way, your ability to write a letter or read a book will not be affected but your attention span may be disrupted.

Diet and Mood Changes in Normal People

The composition of the overall diet and of individual meals has a subtle effect on mood and performance. This differs according to age and sex. After a carbohydrate-rich meal containing less than 10% protein, women tend to feel a little drowsy and men calmer than usual. However, neither effect is significant enough to alter work performance. People over 40, on the other hand, do find it harder to concentrate on work after such a meal. People over 40 also feel more tense after eating a protein-rich meal (one containing more than 50% protein). These effects are consistent with the action of the neurotransmitters involved—high-carbohydrate meals raise brain tryptophan and serotonin levels, and high-protein meals lower them, possible raising brain tyrosine and norepinephrine levels.

Some evidence also shows that marginal deficiencies in the B vitamins and vitamin C can cause symptoms of mild depression and a lack of energy—before these deficiencies show up as real physical problems. Anxiety can also be caused by this type of nutrient shortage. A good one-a-day vitamin supplement containing the RDA (*not* megadoses) is always a wise idea when such deficiencies are suspected and/or meals are not properly balanced. Many people who take medication can suffer from nutrient deficiencies of this type and so can be affected, if they don't take the proper supplements.*

The Right Attitude as Medicine

Researchers have found that the better you feel about life, and the more faith you have in the medications or treatments you are receiving for an ailment, the better you will feel and the better the treatment will work. Until recently, scientists didn't believe that thought processes could influence your

---

*See Appendix 1, "How the Drugs You Take Can Affect Your Brain," pp. 165.

physical health, but now all that has changed. What is popularly called *the hope factor* seems to have a profound affect on the way you feel.

So, along with adjusting your diet to suit particular problems in mood, keep a positive attitude toward life, as much as you can. For whatever esoteric reason, positive-thinking and acting people appear to be healthier and longer-lived than their opposites, and their thinking is clearer. Look on the bright side, and eat on the balanced side.

How to Cope

To raise your mood:
- tryptophan: 2 grams total, taken 3 times a day
- carbohydrates (no more than 10-15 percent of total daily calories (from protein)

OR

- tyrosine: 1-3 grams total, taken 3 times a day
- protein

To get to sleep:
- tryptophan: 1 gram with carbohydrate snack 45-60 minutes before bed.

To alleviate pain:
- tryptophan: 500 mg. total, taken 6 times a day
- carbohydrates

CHAPTER 5

CONTROLLING YOUR APPETITE

You often hear people say, "My stomach is rumbling, let's get something to eat," or "My stomach must have shrunk. I just can't seem to eat as much anymore." We automatically connect the stomach to the concept of hunger, but it is actually the brain that tells you when and when not to eat.

In people who maintain normal weight, it is quite remarkable how their bodies do this. Even though they may eat varying amounts at different times, their weight stays relatively the same. This is partly due to the fact that the brain regulates the appetite and partly because if we ignore its warnings and eat when we are already full, it can make our bodies work less efficiently so that we waste the extra energy we've consumed through the body's expenditure of heat. If our brains didn't do this, every time we ate 3,500 calories over what we need for our daily requirement, we would gain a full pound.

When our brain fails to give us the right signals, or if we ignore the signals, we become overweight or underweight. There are 34 million Americans who are 20 percent or more over their correct weight, and so can be defined as obese. Countless more people wage a continuous battle to keep their weight within the ideal range (see Table 10). Being over-weight is not just a question of aesthetics. It creates an enor-mous psychological burden, and being 5 percent or more over normal weight increases the risk of cancer, heart attack, di-abetes, lung disorders, gout, and arthritis. Conversely, some people have a difficult time motivating themselves to consume enough food to maintain their lowest desirable body weight. Problems that fall into this category, like anorexia and bulimia, are discussed at greater length in this chapter.

The part of the brain that controls the appetite is the hypothalamus. When the level of norepinephrine in the hypothalamus goes up, your appetite increases, and vice versa.* Conversely, an elevation in serotonin levels causes satiety and so serotonin depletion leads to an increased appe-tite. A number of other substances also have an effect on appetite because they affect the hypothalamus, either directly or by changing norepinephrine or serotonin levels. Approx-imately 20 different substances fall into this category, but the most important ones are those which we can manipulate to help control appetite problems.

Glucose and fatty acids (the building blocks of fat) have a direct effect on the hypothalamus; endorphins and amino acids act directly on the hypothalamus as well as on neurotransmitter levels; and several hormones liberated by the gastrointestinal tract also influence neurotransmitter levels.

Short-Term Control of Appetite

The amount of glucose being used by the cells in the hypothalamus is believed to control the appetite between meals. When the level of glucose in the blood drops the glucose available for use by these cells drops and you feel hungry. You may be able to ignore these pangs for a while, but they will eventually become overpowering. If you fast for a day or more, you may end up gorging yourself because of your

---

*The popular over-the-counter diet pills that contain the drug phenylpropanolamine are believed to work by reducing the levels of norepinephrine in the hypothalamus. You should not take more than 50-75 mg. of these drugs daily, because this can cause dangerously elevated blood-pressure levels.

TABLE 10

Recommended Body Weights

MEN

Height (in)	Recommended Weight (lb)	Weight Range (lb)
60	122	102-128
61	126	106-132
62	131	109-136
63	135	113-141
64	139	116-145
65	144	120-150
66	148	124-155
67	152	128-159
68	157	131-164
69	161	135-169
70	166	139-174
71	171	143-179
72	175	147-184
73	179	151-189
74	184	155-194

WOMEN

Height (in)	Recommended Weight (lb)	Weight Range (lb)
58	114	95-129
59	119	99-133
60	121	102-138
61	124	106-142
62	128	109-147
63	131	113-152
64	134	116-157
65	137	120-162
66	140	124-167
67	144	128-172
68	147	131-177
69	150	135-182
70	153	139-187

ravenous hunger, and take in even more calories than you would have by eating normally. Well-spaced meals ensure that your blood glucose levels never fall too far below normal and so few hunger pains result—which is a benefit to dieters. The other type of eating—starving and then overeating—often causes problems in weight loss. Many people complain that they haven't eaten a thing all day, suffered from terrible pangs of hunger, and still gained weight. On closer examination, a nutritionist often finds that the person ate only a few hundred calories during the day but became so ravenous at night that he or she consumed 4,000 calories in one sitting.

Hypoglycemia

For certain people, the attempt to satisfy hunger by eating a sugary snack backfires and they become even hungrier a few hours later. They may also feel weak, anxious, and irritable, may start to tremble and perspire, and their heartbeats may become more rapid than normal. These symptoms are due to a condition known as *hypoglycemia*. Although these symptoms are not long lasting, they are disruptive. Hypoglycemia is caused by the overproduction of insulin by the pancreas, which results in an abnormally rapid drop in blood sugar levels after the consumption and absorption of a lot of sugar. This, of course, reduces the amount of glucose reaching the hypothalamus, causing the ravenous hunger experienced a few hours after eating a candy bar.

It is easiest to explain the difference between a normal and a hypoglycemic person by drawing a simple figure. when a normal person eats sugar, the level of glucose in the blood goes up and then down slowly, like this:

When a hypoglycemia person eats sugar, the rise is the same but the drop is sharp (and even below normal), like this:

Here's the good news: Hypoglycemia is not nearly as common an ailment as some popular writers would have us believe. Many people today are erroneously blaming hypoglycemia for their problems with anxiety or dizziness. Actually, it's a relatively rare problem. But if you do suspect you are hypoglycemic, check with your doctor for a simple test that will tell the tale. If you are diagnosed as hypoglycemic, replace the simple sugars in your diet with complex carbohydrates. The simple sugars are quickly digested and enter the blood stream rapidly, causing sharp increases in blood sugar levels, whereas the complex carbohydrates are more slowly digested and enter the bloodstream gradually, never causing dramatic rises in blood sugar. The higher the blood sugar levels go, the more likely the pancreas is to overreact.

In practical terms, hypoglycemics should avoid all candy, sugar, jellies, jam, desserts, and soft drinks containing sugar. Forty to 45 percent of the dietary calories should be supplied by complex carbohydrates, such as fruits, vegetables, bread, cereals, potatoes, and other starches. Protein should comprise 20%, which means generous servings of meat, fish, poultry, and cheese. The remainder of the daily calories should come from fat. Because milk contains the simple sugar lactose it must be limited to two cups daily. It is best to divide the food into three main meals and three snacks in order to ensure that there is never a large gap between mealtimes. In this way, fluctuations in glucose levels are kept to a minimum. Alcohol should be avoided, since it prevents the liver from producing glucose should blood glucose levels drop below normal. It is also a good idea to carry around some crackers and cheese just in case an attack of hypoglycemia occurs.

The Role of the Stomach in Short-Term Appetite Control

When the stomach is severely distended, as it can be when you eat a very large meal, the stretched walls of the stomach send messages to the hypothalamus that signal satiety. However, this mechanism doesn't work unless the stomach is so full that you feel uncomfortable. There are many dieting "aids" on the market that are essentially indigestible fiber—these products, containing guar gum or pectin, swell as they absorb water in the stomach and thereby stretch it. These same substances can also cause the satiety effect in the intestine in smaller amounts. Products containing cellulose, bran, or other types of fiber are much less effective, as they do not absorb very much water.

Long-Term Appetite Control

Amino Acid Theory

Many theories attempt to explain how the hypothalamus keeps us within our correct weight range. One is that food intake is determined by the levels of amino acids—the building blocks of protein—in the blood supplying the hypothalamus. When these levels drop below a certain point, you become hungry. This may partly explain why so many dieters are successful on high-protein weight-loss plans. People who achieve a quick initial weight loss on these diets feel more encouraged to continue the battle. A diet of 800-1,000 calories a day containing 40% protein, 30% fat, and 30% carbohydrate will indeed cause quick weight loss. However, most of the weight lost in the first two weeks on the diet is water.

Water loss leads to potassium depletion and can be damaging to the heart, and so any dieter on this type of plan should be sure to include good sources of potassium in his or her meals and try to avoid foods rich in sodium, which will exacerbate the potassium losses.

As food passes down the digestive tract, a number of hormones are liberated, including *cholecystokinin, somatosta-tin*, and *glucagon*, which tend to decrease norepinephrine levels in the hypothalamus, so decreasing hunger. Two amino acids—tryptophan and phenylalanine*—if taken in large doses (10 grams distributed throughout the day, taken 5 to 15 minutes after the onset of meals) have been shown to elevate cholecystokinin levels in some people, decreasing the appetite. This may be another reason why people on high-protein diets tend to feel less hungry.

Set Point Theory

Another of the most widely acknowledged theories of appetite control maintains that the hypothalamus stimulates the appetite in such a way as to maintain the level of body fat at a set point or constant level.

If you give a non-domesticated animal all it wants to eat, it will eat just enough to maintain its body weight. If you force-feed such an animal it will get fatter, but the moment the force-feeding is stopped its food intake will decrease below normal and its weight will return to normal. If it is semi-starved it will lose weight, but when given free access to food its food intake will increase above normal and its weight will return to normal again. This stable weight is called the set point.

Body fat is made up of millions of individual fat cells. Most fat cells are acquired during early childhood and adolescence, but small increases can occur at any time in your life. However, once these fat cells are acquired you can never lose them. Fat cell size is elastic and depends on how much fat is stored within the cell (the main way the body stores energy).

Fat cells are continuously releasing fatty acids into the bloodstream. These substances are absorbed by the other tissues and turned into energy. As you might expect, during a fast, larger quantities of fatty acids are pumped into the bloodstream. As the level of fatty acids passing through the hypothalamus increases, the hypothalamus is triggered to increase the appetite. As the fat cells liberate fatty acids they become

---

*Warning: Pregnant women should not take phenylalanine since it can cause mental retardation in susceptible infants.

progressively smaller and body weight declines. When a person begins to eat again, the excess calories are stored as fat in the fat cells. However, the fat cells continue to liberate higher-than-normal amounts of fatty acids until they return to their prefasting size, which means that the appetite is maintained at a higher level until the fat cells regain normal size and the body returns to its fixed point. In order to facilitate this process the hypothalamus sends messages, directly via the nerves and indirectly via the hormonal system, to the various tissues in the body to make them conserve energy.

People who have a weight problem usually have more and larger fat cells than naturally lean people. In fact, their cells may be as much as two-and-a-half times as large. It is this extra mass of fat cells that makes them heavy. If they reduce their fat cell size by dieting they will still be overweight because they

---

TABLE 11

Good Food Sources of Potassium

FOOD	SERVING SIZE	POTASSIUM (mg)
Apricots, dried	1 cup	1,273
Avocado, Florida	1	1,836
Banana	1 small	440
Beans, lima	1 cup	740
Brussels sprouts, fresh cooked	1 cup	423
Carrots, cooked	1 cup	344
Chicken, broiled	6 ounces	483
Clams, soft	3 ounces	225
Dates, pitted	10	518
Flounder	6 ounces	1,000
Milk, skim	1 cup	406
Orange juice	1 cup	496
Potato, baked	1 medium	782
Prunes, dried and pitted	5 large	298
Spinach, chopped and cooked	1 cup	688
Sweetbreads	3 ounces	433
Tomato, raw	1 medium	300
Tuna, salt-free, canned	1 small container	327
Yogurt, plain	1 container	531

TABLE 12

Food Sources of Sodium

FOOD	SERVING	SODIUM (mg)
Bacon	3 ounces	875
Baked beans	1 cup	862
Beans, lima	1 cup	192
Beets, canned	1 cup	378
Bread, cracked wheat	1 slice	132
Bread, raisin	1 slice	91
Bread, rye	1 slice	139
Bread, white	1 slice	127
Bread, whole wheat	1 slice	148
Butter, salted	1 ounce	282
Buttermilk	1 cup	319
Cheese, cheddar	2 ounces	400
Cheese, creamed cottage	2 ounces	131
Cheese, parmesan	2 ounces	419
Chicken	4 ounces	73-98
Clams	4 ounces	137
Corn, canned	1 cup	496
Corn, sweet	1 cup	25
Cornflakes	1 ounce	287
Crab	4 ounces	1,140
Egg	1 medium	61
Fish	4 ounces	125-202
Ham	4 ounces	1,063
Liver	4 ounces	210
Lobster	4 ounces	239
Margarine, regular	1 ounce	282
Margarine, unsalted	1 ounce	3
Olives, green	4 medium	384
Peanut butter	1 ounce	173
Peas, canned	1 cup	401
Pickles, dill	1	857
Pickles, sweet	1	79
Pretzels	1	269
Salad dressing	1 tablespoon	96-335

have so many more cells. The only way they can weigh the same as a lean person is to reduce their fat cell size below normal. But as we explained, when the fat cell size is reduced below normal the quantity of fatty acids released is elevated, causing an increase in appetite. This is why people who are always on a diet feel hungry most of the time even when they get down to their ideal weight. The energy conservation mechanism works very well in these people, as this is also turned on when the size of their fat cells decreases to a point below their normal size. For this reason they have to consume fewer calories to maintain normal weight than naturally lean people (this difference can be as great as 25 percent).

A few years ago a study examined this phenomenon. Several naturally lean people, along with several people with weight problems who had recently dieted down to a normal weight, took part in the study. Both groups were of roughly the same weight. The lean group maintained weight on a diet of about 2,500 calories a day, but the previously overweight group was able to eat no more than 1,000 calories—and one member maintained weight on 600 calories a day. This is one reason why 66% of all frequent dieters gain back the weight they have lost when they go off the diet. Even if they consume no more calories than is normal for someone of their height and weight, they will gain weight. And even if they can control their appetites, their caloric need will remain below normal for the rest of their lives, since at their ideal body weight they are actually below their fixed point.

It is just as difficult for naturally lean people to gain weight and keep it on. In the same study, the lean subjects were given 6,000 calories a day for a two-month period. Since this group maintained their weight on 2,500 calories, they were now consuming an extra 3,500 calories each day. Theoretically, for every 3,500 calories you consume over and above what you need for your energy requirements, you should gain one pound in body fat. Hence, the lean group should have gained 56 pounds during the experimental period. Yet many gained no weight at all, and the average gain in the group was only five pounds. Within a month after the end of the study, everybody in the lean group was back to his or her normal weight. In this group, throughout the study, the hypothalamus caused their bodies to use energy inefficiently—that is, it caused their bodies to use up an abnormally high amount of energy—and after the study it caused a reduced appetite coupled with this decreased energy use in order to maintain the set points of the lean group.

The Desire for Specific Foods

If you give an animal a choice of two diets, one containing all the essential nutrients and one missing one or more nutrients, after trying both, it will eat only the complete diet. This is because it will feel unwell when it selects the incomplete diet and will learn to select the diet that contains everything it needs for good health. People are no different, and if placed in a room away from newspapers, books, TV sets, or other things that can influence food choices, those who are naturally lean will select a fairly balanced diet. However, many people have cravings for specific foods due to an imbalance in the hypothalamus.

Fat Cravers

People who are overweight show a definite preference for foods that are high in fat and carbohydrate, and have less of a liking for protein. The craving for fatty foods is thought to be caused by higher brain endorphin levels. Endorphins are one of the major appetite stimulators, especially influencing the appetite for fatty foods. They act directly on the hypothalamus, as well as indirectly by raising its norepinephrine levels.

Obese animals were found to have higher levels of endorphins in their hypothalamus and larger appetites. When drugs like naloxone (which neutralizes the effects of endorphins) are given to them, their appetite decreases and their food preferences change away from fatty foods to foods high in protein. Mild stress sometimes increases appetite in animals and when it does, it also raises endorphin levels.

A successful diet must take into account this desire for fatty foods; 30% of the calories in such a reducing diet should come from fat.

Carbohydrate Cravers

One large group of overweight people, along with people of

average weight, show strong and frequent cravings for carbohydrate-rich foods, accompanied by a state of mild depression (see Chapter 4). One study showed that as many as 78% of all overweight women have such cravings, which are aggravated by stress and especially by premenstrual tension. These people eat normally at mealtimes but snack frequently between meals on cookies, candies, or cakes. They also tend to take these snacks at set points during the day, which differ in each person. This pattern is believed to be caused by an inadequate amount of serotonin in the brain and by a learned desire for foods that will boost serotonin levels. It's easy to consume too many calories in this way and gain weight. Drugs like fenfluramine or tryptophan supplements can elevate brain serotonin levels and reduce the need for high-carbohydrate snacks. The proper dose of tryptophan is up to one gram three times a day, equally spaced throughout the waking hours between meals.

Hyperactivity

It has clearly been demonstrated that children are born with a sweet tooth. It is also a commonly held belief that satisfying this desire by eating lots of sugary foods causes or exacerbates hyperactivity in susceptible children either by the direct effect of sugar on the brain or by causing hypoglycemia. However, although a few hyperactive children seem to become worse when given sugar, most experience a calming effect. Therefore, there is little evidence to support the idea that sugar is a major cause of hyperactivity.

Even for the children who do seem to be sensitive to sugar, it has been shown that as long as they take some protein into their bodies along with the sugar they do not show increased hyperactivity. This means that these children do not have to be deprived of desserts or candy, as long as they are consumed within two hours of a meal containing some protein-rich foods.

Anorexia, Overeating, and Depression

Anorexia, or a reduced desire to eat, is characteristic of many nutritional deficiencies, but it also accompanies many illnesses. As discussed in Chapter 4, the most widely accepted theory of depression is that it is caused by a deficiency either of norepinephrine or serotonin. Depressions that are mainly associated with low norepinephrine levels are also connected to anorexia and weight loss, whereas depressions associated with serotonin disturbance are marked by carbohydrate hunger and a subsequent weight gain.

Anorexia Nervosa

It is also interesting to note that low levels of norepinephrine show up in patients with anorexia nervosa, a psychological condition that results in a drastic reduction in food intake and body weight, not related to any other disease state.

Ninety-six percent of anorectics are between the ages of 12 and 30, and 9 out of 10 are female. The fear of puberty, peer pressure, parental pressure, an exaggerated accent on one's appearance, academic pressures, or marriage—all potentially stressful events—can trigger the onset of the disease. In slightly older women, the birth of a first child, career change, divorce, or even menopause can cause the condition.

The prevalence of this illness has increased rapidly over recent years, possible caused by the popular fad that "thin is in." Anorectic patients have usually been overweight at some point in their lives and initially reduced in order to get back to an ideal weight. But this dieting becomes an obsession, and the patients live in irrational fear of regaining any weight. The dieting can go to such extremes that some anorectic patients get their weight down to 70 pounds, and even then fail to accept the fact that they are underweight. When asked to estimate the width of their hips they may overestimate by as much as 50% and select clothes that are many sizes too big for them.

Anorectic patients usually feel hungry, but actively suppress their appetite. After a while the women stop menstruating, and both sexes suffer from a slowed pulse rate, low blood pressure, low body temperature, and hyperactivity. Their mental performance also deteriorates—possible due to decreased blood glucose levels.

Several of these symptoms are due to abnormalities in the functioning of the hypothalamus, and some researchers feel that anorexia results from a primary hypothalamic disorder.

Anorectics show a preference for protein-rich foods. Depression also shows up in those with anorexia nervosa, particularly in the older patients, due to low levels of norepinephrine. It is tempting to believe that anorexia itself is due to low norepinephrine levels and that patients unconsciously select protein-rich foods in an effort to boost these levels, as in the opposite situation with carbohydrate cravers. If this were the case (and it is certainly not proven) then tyrosine supplements might be beneficial, although they could not correct the disorder to any significant degree.

There have been several reports linking a deficiency in zinc to anorexia, and there is a sound scientific basis for using zinc in treatment. Starvation increases urinary excretion of zinc, exacerbating the effect of a shortage of dietary zinc. Estrogen also enhances zinc excretion, and so females past the age of puberty are at special risk, especially those who use oral contraceptives. As the body's zinc levels decline, the impairment of the zinc-dependent senses of taste and smell may be expected to further reduce the desire for food. The minimum effective supplement is 15 to 20 mg. of zinc, as zinc sulfate (50-75 mg in this form). (More than this should not be taken, as too much zinc can be toxic.)

Bulimia

Anorectic patients often go through successive bouts of starvation and then overeating (often followed by self-induced vomiting or the abuse of laxatives and/or diuretics). A separate condition has now been defined as bulimia, describing people of any body weight—from severely starved to above normal—who go on uncontrolled eating binges followed by self-induced purging. Bulimics tend to eat sweet, high-calorie foods, such as ice cream, candy, and donuts. Binges last less than two hours and are often done in secret. Binge and purge episodes can occur once a day, once a week, or less frequently.

This condition is again more common in young women suffering from depression or a low sense of self-esteem—in fact, 90% are female. They often suffer from chronic indigestion, facial puffiness, menstrual disturbances, sore throats, cardiac arrhythmias due to potassium deficiency, vitamin and mineral deficiencies of many types, and erosion of the teeth (caused by the acid brought up from the stomach during the self-induced vomiting).

Although it is again tempting to suggest that the preference shown by these people for high-carbohydrate foods and their characteristic depression is reminiscent of carbohydrate cravers, there is no concrete evidence that low serotonin levels are the cause of the disease. In fact, the cause remains unknown.

Treatment for both anorectics and bulimics involves help from psychiatrists, internists, and nutritionists, and the conditions should not be ignored. Six percent of all people suffering from anorexia nervosa die of starvation, and many bulimics commit suicide. We hope that in the future these conditions are pinpointed to a particular brain dysfunction and can be treated successfully with simple supplements or medications.

In Conclusion

The control of appetite and body weight is a complex issue. A huge number of factors affect the functioning of the hypothalamus, and so influence feelings of hunger or satiety. In fact, it is the balance of all these different factors that determines the outcome. For instance, we know from previous chapters that high-protein diets elevate brain norepinephrine levels, and earlier in this chapter we explained that high hypothalamic levels of norepinephrine lead to an increased appetite. Then, why do so many dieters find success by following a high-protein diet? The reason is that all the other factors mentioned in this chapter outweigh the increased norepinephrine levels.

As you can see, the control of body weight is not just a matter of willpower or poor eating habits. Again, it is the domain of the brain. However, we can help ourselves by eating balanced meals, trying to keep to our ideal weight, and recognizing when we do have a weight problem so that we can adjust our eating habits to correct it.

How to Cope

If you are hypoglycemic:
- Avoid sugar
- Diet should consist of 45 percent complex carbohydrates, 20 percent protein, and 35 percent fat
- Limit milk to 2 cups

If you crave carbohydrates:
- Tryptophan: 250mg–1 gram, taken 3 times a day between meals

If you are anorexic:
- Zinc sulfate: 50-75 mg per day.

CHAPTER 6

FOR WOMEN ONLY: PMS

Queen Victoria was well known for her emotional outbursts. She would suddenly scream at people for no apparent reason and at times would even throw things at them—especially at her husband, Prince Albert. What was interesting about these scenes was that they seemed to occur in a cyclical pattern; only when the Queen was pregnant was she free of this irrational behavior.

It is quite possible, from what scientists know today, that Queen Victoria was suffering from PMS, or premenstrual syndrome. Cramps, headaches, bloating, depression, anxiety—all these symptoms were once considered the normal side-effects of a woman's menstrual cycle. But researchers now believe that no form of pain or discomfort can be considered "normal" for the body and that such problems signal instead a physical imbalance caused by certain chemical irregularities in the body and/or dietary deficiencies.

PMS mainly affects a woman a week or so before her menstrual period and during the first few days of bleeding. It can be marked by some positive changes, such as increased energy, heightened sexual desire, or feelings of well-being, as well as more than 150 negative changes.

A woman with PMS may suffer from any combination of these symptoms. The severity varies from one woman to another and tends to increase with age, until, for some reason, PMS can become almost unmanageable. And though PMS in its most common forms is not linked to any other major illness, it can lead to tragedy. Statistics show that more women commit suicide just prior to their menstrual periods than at any other time in the month. PMS is now accepted in certain countries as a legal defense. In Britain it was used to reduce one woman's

---

TABLE 13

Common Symptoms Experienced by Women with PMS

Accident proneness	Fuzzy vision
Anger	General aches and pains
Anxiety	Headaches
Avoidance of social activities	Heart pounding
Backache	Hot flashes
Blind spots	Increased appetite
Chest pains	Insomnia
Cold sweats	Irritability
Confusion	Lethargy
Constipation	Loneliness
Cramps	Mood swings
Craving for salt	Muscle stiffness
Craving for sweets	Nausea
Crying	Numbness and tingling in limbs
Decreased efficiency	Obsession with order
Depression	Pain in the breasts
Desire to take naps and	Poor coordination
stay in bed	Poor judgement
Diarrhea	Respiratory problems
Dizziness	Restlessness
Dull aches	Ringing in the ears
Easily distracted	Skin problems
Excitability	Swelling in the breasts
Faintness	Swelling in the joints
Fatigue	Tenseness
Feelings of suffocation	Vomiting
Forgetfulness	

---

conviction for murder to manslaughter; in France it is now considered grounds for a plea of temporary insanity. Approximately 30 percent of all women of child-bearing age are now believed to suffer from some adverse symptoms of PMS. The highest-risk women are:

- married
- have more than one child
- older
- those who eat an unbalanced diet
- those who consume a lot of sugar, salt, and caffeine
- those who get little or no exercise
- heavy alcohol or drug users
- heavy smokers

No one knows for sure what causes PMS, but most experts feel that it has something to do with hormonal imbalances occurring during the menstrual cycle. An imbalance could be the result of disturbed rhythms in the hypothalamus and/or the pituitary, which control the hormonal system of the body, including the sex hormones estrogen and progesterone. An excess of either estrogen or progesterone in relation to the other may be responsible for the changes experienced by PMS sufferers. Many doctors treat PMS by prescribing progesterone.

Despite a lack of sound scientific data, 60 percent of all physicians treating PMS also recommend some kind of dietary modification or supplement, and sometimes exercise. Many women experience relief after making such dietary changes. As medical science cannot offer relief of all PMS symptoms at the present time, improving your diet is certainly worth trying. It will not do any harm, and it may indeed help.

Safe and Plausible Dietary Therapies for PMS

Carbohydrate Cravers

A large number of women suffer from carbohydrate craving associated with premenstrual depression. As discussed in Chapter 4, these two symptoms are often associated with low brain serotonin levels. Therefore, one-half to one gram of tryptophan taken three times a day with a carbohydrate-rich snack such as cookies or cake or sweetened beverage like fruit juice or soda, could be helpful.

Women with Hypoglycemia

A tendency to develop hypoglycemia is not uncommon among PMS sufferers. If you experience cold sweats, dizziness, faintness, headaches, and heart-pounding two to four hours after eating foods containing sugar, you could be hypoglycemic in this way, due to abnormal hormonal changes that cause an increased secretion of insulin after sweet foods are eaten. You should follow the advice offered to hypoglycemics in Chapter 5—avoid simple sugars and replace them with complex carbohydrates, and eat little but often. Alcohol should be avoided because it prevents the liver from producing glucose should blood glucose levels fall below normal.

Vitamin B_6 and Magnesium Deficiencies

Magnesium and vitamin B_6 are essential to the brain. They enable it to produce the neurotransmitters serotonin and dopamine. A deficiency in either nutrient (or both) could be responsible for the psychological changes seen in PMS, such as mood swings and depression. Several studies have shown low magnesium levels in PMS sufferers.

One out of every two Americans consumes less than the RDA for B6 (2-3 mg.). Women taking oral contraceptives are especially at risk for B_6 deficiency, as the estrogen in these pills stimulates many reactions in the body that require B_6, and also makes the vitamin work less efficiently. It has been observed that 15 to 20 percent of oral contraceptive users are B_6-deficient. Many physicians believe that such deficiencies, by reducing brain serotonin levels, account for such PMS symptoms as insomnia, increased appetite, headaches, depression, and various aches and pains. It is advisable, then, that *all* women who take the pill also take a daily supplement of five milligrams of vitamin B_6. Women with PMS who are most likely to benefit from B_6 supplements are those with a history of depression whose depression increased when put on oral contraceptives.

If you drink or smoke you also need more B_6. There are 2 million female alcoholics in the reproductive age group in

TABLE 14

Good Food Sources of Vitamin B$_6$

FOOD	SERVING	VITAMIN B$_6$ (mg)
Bananas	1 medium	.61
Beef	4 ounces	.30
Bran flakes	1 cup	.29
Cabbage, cooked	1 cup	.10
Carrots, cooked	1 cup	.10
Fish	4 ounces	.23-.95
Grape-Nuts cereal	3 ounces	2.41
Lamb	4 ounces	.14
Liver	4 ounces	.83
Milk	1 cup	.10
Oatmeal	1 cup	.29
Peanuts	1 cup	.58
Pork	4 ounces	.47
Potato, baked	1 medium	.28
Veal	4 ounces	.36

the U.S. Out of these, 67 percent relate their drinking to the menstrual cycle. Drinking bouts almost always occur in the week prior to menstruation, probably to relieve anxiety. A low daily intake of alcohol (one drink hard liquor, one or two glasses of wine, or one beer) should not be a problem, provided your dietary intake of B$_6$ equals the RDA.

To prevent any PMS symptoms due to inadequate dietary B$_6$, you should take a 25-50 mg. supplement of the vitamin every day. However, do not take too much more, as a daily intake of 250 mg. has been reported to cause neurological disorders. If you see no improvement after taking the supplement through three complete monthly cycles, discontinue it. In any case, be certain that you are getting enough of the vitamin through your diet.

TABLE 15

Food Sources of Magnesium

FOOD	SERVING SIZE	MAGNESIUM (mg)
Almonds	1 ounce	77
Avocado	3 ounces	39
Beet greens, raw	1 cup	154
Bran	1 ounce	140
Brazil nuts	1 ounce	65
Cashews	1 ounce	76
Cereal, whole grain	1 ounce	38
Cheese	2 ounces	27
Chocolate	2 ounces	167
Hazelnuts	1 ounce	53
Lima beans	1 cup	91
Peanuts	1 ounce	50
Pecans	1 ounce	41
Pistachios	1 ounce	45
Shrimp	4 ounces	58
Soybean curd	3 ounces	95
Spinach, cooked	1 cup	113
Walnuts	1 ounce	37
Wheat germ	1 ounce	96

In addition, it is important to get enough magnesium. A deficiency of this mineral can contribute to depression, lethargy and confusion. You need 300 mg. daily and so you should either change your diet accordingly, or take a 200-300 mg. supplement. Avoid heavy alcohol consumption, which causes the body to excrete a lot of magnesium through the urine.

Water Retention

Fluid retention (edema) is one of the main complaints of PMS sufferers. This may take the form of swelling in the breasts, genitals, joints, or abdomen. Some doctors believe that fluid retention in the brain may be another cause of PMS's psychological effects. Although the primary cause of edema is thought to be due to hormonal imbalances, it has been shown that a diet high in sodium can make the condition worse. Many people are not even aware of how much sodium they eat. Each teaspoon of salt in the diet contains two grams of sodium. Sodium can also be found in other compounds in the diet, such as monosodium glutamate. If salt (sodium chloride) or any compound containing sodium appears as one of the first ingredients on a food label, then the product contains a significant amount. If, on the other hand, it appears very near the end of the list (as with bread), there is no need for concern.

PMS sufferers with edema should cut back on their sodium intake to about three grams a day. This means that no salt should be added at the table, but up to one teaspoon per day can be added during cooking. In addition, avoid very salty foods, such as luncheon meats, chips, canned soups and vegetables, TV dinners, soy sauce, processed cheeses, and pickled foods, like sauerkraut. *Table 16* lists other foods that are rich in sodium and should be used in moderation.

Aerobic exercise is also beneficial because it helps to dissipate the fluid retained in the tissues. Swimming is a particularly good choice. Exercise also helps relieve stress and tension, possibly by raising brain endorphin levels.

Prostaglandins

Prostaglandins are chemicals naturally found in the body, which are believed to correct hormonal abnormalities in women with PMS, so relieving the symptoms. Prostaglandins are made from linoleic acid found in vegetable oils (safflower oil is an excellent source and should be used to replace any other type of fats normally used in food preparation). Your body needs vitamins B_6 and C, niacin, and zinc to make prostaglandins and so you should include in your diet plenty of foods rich in these nutrients, or take a daily vitamin and mineral supplement containing the RDA.*

---

* B_6 = 2-3 mg.; C = 60-100 mg.; niacin = 20 mg.; zinc = 15 mg.

TABLE 16

Food Sources of Sodium

FOOD	SERVING	SODIUM (mg)
Bacon	3 ounces	875
Baked beans	1 cup	862
Beans, lima	1 cup	192
Beets, canned	1 cup	378
Bread, cracked wheat	1 slice	132
Bread, raisin	1 slice	91
Bread, rye	1 slice	139
Bread, white	1 slice	127
Bread, whole wheat	1 slice	148
Butter, salted	1 ounce	282
Buttermilk	1 cup	319
Cheese, cheddar	2 ounces	400
Cheese, creamed cottage	2 ounces	131
Cheese, parmesan	2 ounces	419
Chicken	4 ounces	73-98
Clams	4 ounces	137
Corn, canned	1 cup	496
Corn, sweet	1 cup	25
Cornflakes	1 ounce	287
Crab	4 ounces	1,140
Egg	1 medium	61
Fish	4 ounces	125-202
Ham	4 ounces	1,063
Liver	4 ounces	210
Lobster	4 ounces	239
Margarine, regular	1 ounce	282
Margarine, unsalted	1 ounce	3
Olives, green	4 medium	384
Peanut butter	1 ounce	173
Peas, canned	1 cup	401
Pickles, dill	1	857
Pickles, sweet	1	79
Pretzels	1	269
Salad dressing	1 tablespoon	96-335

Caffeine

Many people believe that caffeine exacerbates the breast-affecting symptoms of PMS. But recent evidence shows that it makes *all* symptoms of the condition worse. In a study involving over 200 college-age women, the prevalence and severity of PMS increased with a greater intake of caffeine-containing beverages. The reason for this is not yet known. However, sufferers should cut out or limit caffeine for a trial period of three monthly cycles to see if they notice any improvement in their symptoms. Foods and beverages high in caffeine include coffee, tea, colas, chocolate, and many cough and analgesic medications.

PMS: An Overview

It is sad that so little research has been done to date on PMS, considering that the condition has been noted for several hundred years. We still do not know what causes it and have not found a proven cure. Although nutritional cures are not backed up by a wealth of research, many women seem to benefit from them and they are certainly safe. Many of the recommendations outlined here—increasing complex carbohydrates, decreasing salt and sugar intake, and replacing saturated fat with vegetable oils in food preparation—are the ones nutritionists and physicians endorse to ensure good health for everyone, PMS sufferers or not. As far as PMS goes, first make sure that you do have it—many other health problems are connected with the symptoms listed on p. 80. If you do have PMS, the symptoms will be cyclical, appearing at the same time every month and becoming most severe during the week before and at the start of your period. They should be gone, or at least very mild, the week after the end of your period. If you don't have PMS, you may have another, more serious illness causing these symptoms and so you should check with your doctor.

HOW TO COPE

To lessen carbohydrates craving with depression:
- 1/2-1 gram tryptophan, taken 3 times a day

If you are hypoglycemic:
- eliminate sugar
- avoid alcohol
- eat little, but often

To alleviate insomnia, depression, aches and pains, and to decrease appetite:
- vitamin B_6: 30mg.
- magnesium: 300mg. from food
- cut back alcohol consumption

To decrease water retention:
- reduce dietary sodium to 3 grams
- aerobic exercise

To increase prostaglandins:
- use vegetable oils (especially safflower oil) in cooking
- get RDA of vitamin B_6 (2-3 mg.), vitamin C (60-100 mg.), niacin (20 mg.), and zinc (15 mg.)

CHAPTER 7

LEARNING AND REMEMBERING

The finest and most subtle qualities of the human mind lie in its ability to think and reason—in other words, its intellect. But the exact nature of intelligence, and how it differs from person to person, has eluded modern science despite the widespread belief in the exactitude of such devices as IQ tests, a belief that is now beginning to crumble, and rightly so.

However, we do know that the food we eat affects our intellectual performance. What we eat, as well as when we eat it, has an effect on how well we think. In addition, the ability to remember can be aided by the right nutritional supplements.

How Meals Affect Your Mental Performance

Both the skipping of meals and the consumption of heavy meals appear to have a significant effect on how a person performs mentally. Skipping breakfast, for example, influences how well a child does at school. Children who do not eat breakfast, or who eat the wrong kinds of foods, perform noticeably poorer than children who are well-nourished in the morning. As the morning wears on, the children without breakfast perform less and less well. This is thought to be caused by a drop in blood glucose levels. Children with above average intelligence seem to be able to compensate to some extent and are less affected than the others, but it is still a problem.

The composition of the breakfast is very important. The children who do the best are those whose morning meal is balanced in protein, carbohydrate, and fat—such as cereal and milk, egg, toast, and orange juice. Children who eat cookies, sugary cereals, and cake do not perform as well, although they do better than those who miss the meal totally. (However, sugar-sensitive hyperactive children are better off not eating breakfast than having one composed of sweet foods.)

Adults also experience changes in mental performance following breakfast and lunch. The factors important here include the quantity of food eaten, the composition of the meal (such as the ratio of carbohydrate to protein), the time of day the meal is eaten, the characteristics of the person her- or himself, and the complexity of the mental tasks performed (the more difficult the job, the greater the effect will be).

As with children, a missed meal impairs an adult's mental performance. As the morning wears on, an office worker who has missed breakfast will make more and more mistakes than one who has not. By about 11 A.M., the difference will be considerable. On the other end of the scale, an excessively heavy meal can be just as harmful, especially for someone who doesn't normally eat that much. For example, if you usually eat a sandwich for lunch (400 calories) and one day go out for a full business lunch (1,000 calories or more) you may very well experience extreme sluggishness after the meal, and find yourself making many more mistakes in your work than usual. In fact, it has been shown that this type of situation has comparable effects on mental behavior as not having slept the whole night before—which reduces your mental ability by as much as 10 percent. This effect will persist for two or three hours after the heavy meal. It is made even worse by the fact that many people tend to become slightly tired at about 2 P.M., and their thinking becomes less sharp, no matter what they have or have not eaten.

Recent experiments conducted in England showed that pilots who were fed a heavy lunch, and who normally ate a light one, suffered from significantly impaired vision. The overall point is that any unusual change in eating habits may have a harmful effect on mental performance. The time of day doesn't matter; night-shift workers would be similarly affected if they changed their normal eating patterns.

However, in some situations, the potential effect of a meal on mental performance can be a matter of the lesser of two evils. If a person has not eaten for a long time (24 hours or more), the effect of being ravenously hungry is more harmful than if he or she was then to consume a large meal. It is better in this case, for the sake of mental performance, to stuff than to starve.

What a meal consists of is also crucial. A high-carbohydrate, low-protein meal will make it more difficult for your brain to concentrate and process information. You would find it harder to remember a mental shopping list, play chess, or do your work. However, it will not impair your reactions. Your ability to make an emergency stop in a car, for example, would still be normal. Although anyone can suffer from this problem, people over the age of 40 show the strongest effect, and more so in the afternoon than in the morning.

Personality also plays a significant part in your reaction to a meal. Very stable people and extroverts—who are very influenced by external situations—are more vulnerable to the effects of a change in dietary habits than someone who is neurotic or introverted. The total mechanism operating behind this difference is not yet fully understood.

Iron Deficiency and Mental Performance

Many nutrient deficiencies impair mental performance, as we saw in Chapter 2. However, one of these—iron deficiency—probably affects more people in our society in this way than any other type. Many reports suggest that iron deficiency, which causes the brain to get less of the oxygen it needs to produce energy, decreases attention span, affects concentration, and can cause irritability and headaches. It should be mentioned that no one has proved that a poor iron status actually decreases the intellect—just the performance.

In recent years it has been shown that measurement of the brain's electrical activity provides an accurate indication of intellect. This procedure has demonstrated that the lower the iron stores in adults, the less alert they are, and the poorer they perform in mental work. This is an important finding—it means a person doesn't have to be anemic to be affected. Iron stores must be kept at top levels for peak mental performance. In the U.S., 10 percent of all premenopausal women are believed to be iron-deficient, and 30 percent have less than optimal stores. Many male teenagers and elderly people of both sexes also show a poor iron status. As you can see, we are describing a serious potential problem for large numbers of people. To have the best possible physical stores of iron, women need 18 mg. a day, and men 10 mg. (see *Table 17* for a list of foods rich in iron).

The reason for this phenomenon is unclear. It could be that a reduction in iron levels in the body means that there is less

TABLE 17

Good Food Sources of Iron

FOOD	SERVING	IRON (mg)
Amaranth	3 1/2 ounces	2.0 - 4.0
Apricots, dried	6 large halves	1.5 - 2.0
Barley	1/2 cup	1.5 - 2.0
Beans, green	1 cup	1.5 - 2.0
Beans, cooked	1/2 cup	2.0 - 4.0
Beef, lean	3 ounces	4.0 - 5.0
Berries	1 cup	0.7 - 1.4
Bologna	3 to 4 ounces	1.5 - 2.0
Bread	1 slice	0.3 - 0.7
Brewer's yeast	1 tablespoon	1.5 - 2.0
Broccoli	1 cup	0.7 - 1.4
Buckwheat	1/2 cup	1.5 - 2.0
Bulgur wheat, dry	2 tablespoons	0.7 - 1.4
Calf's liver	1 ounce	4.0 - 5.0
Carrots	1 cup	0.7 - 1.4
Chicken	3 to 4 ounces	1.5 - 2.0
Collards	1 cup	0.7 - 1.4
Corn grits	1 cup	0.3 - 0.7
Cream of wheat	1 cup	0.7 - 1.4
Eggplant	1/2 cup	0.3 - 0.7
Figs, dried	3 medium	2.0 - 4.0

available to work as cofactors in the brain's production of neurotransmitters, including dopamine, norepinephrine, and serotonin. On the other hand, it could mean that the less iron you consume the more lead gets into your body, and lead is known to reduce the intellect. Animal studies have shown that dietary iron deficiency can result in the increased absorption by the body of several metals, including lead, cadmium, and iron. Lead is found in the atmosphere from car exhaust fumes and industrial pollution, in paint, and in the food we eat— mainly from the material used to seal cans. (Foods should never be left in cans once they have been opened, as large amounts of lead leach out into the food upon exposure to the air.)

TABLE 17 (continued)

FOOD	SERVING	IRON (mg)
Fruits, including apples bananas, cherries, citrus, melons, pineapple, etc.	1 piece	0.3 - 0.7
Ham	2 ounces	1.5 - 2.0
Lamb, lean	4 ounces	4.0 - 5.0
Molasses, blackstrap	1 tablespoon	2.0 - 4.0
Mushrooms	1/3 cup	0.3 - 0.7
Oatmeal	1 cup	1.5 - 2.0
Pasta	1/2	0.3 - 0.7
Peanut butter	2 tablespoons	0.3 - 0.7
Peas	1/2 cup	2.0 - 4.0
Popcorn	1 cup	0.3 - 0.7
Potato	1 medium	0.7 - 1.4
Pumpkin seeds	1 to 2 tablespoons	0.7 - 1.4
Raisins	1/2 cup	4.0 - 5.0
Rice, white or brown	1 cup	0.7 - 1.4
Tomato	1 small	0.3 - 0.7
Soybean curd	4 ounces	2.0 - 4.0
Tortilla	(approx. 6 inches)	0.7 - 1.4
Wheatena	2/3 cup	0.7 - 1.4

Several studies have shown that there is an association between high body cadmium levels and learning disabilities. Cadmium exposure comes from drinking water coming through galvanized pipes, from refined flour, and from vegetables grown in soil containing a high cadmium level, many processed foods, many plastics, and cigarette smoke. As you can see, it is impossible to eliminate your exposure to lead or cadmium, but you can be safe from any ill effects by getting enough iron through your diet.

Can Memory Be Improved?

Within our long- and short-term memories is everything that has happened to us. But the memory provides us with even more than that. Through the storage of this learned data we make conclusions, act on similar circumstances, learn new skills, and build a library of knowledge to be used for everyday reference.

The neurotransmitter acetylcholine appears to be responsible for the acquisition of new information, whereas norepinephrine takes responsibility for the storage of this information for long-term use.

It is hard to improve long-term memory, and we do not yet know if changing the levels of norepinephrine influences it. However, short-term memory, which is responsible for learning, does appear to be affected by the administration of choline, which helps to raise acetylcholine levels in the brain. Two studies conducted at the National Institute of Mental Health, involving normal people in their twenties, showed that a single dose of 10 grams of choline chloride improved their performance on a task involving memory only 90 minutes after the substance was taken. Those with the poorest memories improved the most.

Choline taken in this form, however, is not fully absorbed into the body, and the bacteria in the intestines convert it to trimethylamine, which gives the feces an unpleasant odor. For this reason, lecithin (which does not have this side effect) is a better source of choline. Approximately 30 grams of lecithin contains the same amount of choline as 10 grams of choline chloride—buy only the lecithin called phosphatidylcholine, because most other products going under the label of lecithin

TABLE 18

Good Food Sources of Lecithin or Choline Chloride (mg. per 100 grams)*

FOOD SOURCE	LECITHIN	CHOLINE CHLORIDE
Beef	453	
Calf's liver	850	650
Canadian Bacon	533	
Egg	394	
Ham	800	
Lamb	753	
Oatmeal	650	131
Peanuts	1113	
Red Snapper	560	
Soy beans	1480	
Trout	580	
Veal	880	
Wheat bran	953	
Wheat germ	2820	
White Rice	580	

*(28 grams is equivalent to one ounce)

contain impurities and hence less choline per gram.

Thirty grams is a lot to take. This is one of the problems with using lecithin to improve memory. Lecithin is a form of fat, which means that every gram is equivalent to nine calories, and so 30 grams equals 270 calories. If you consider that a cheese sandwich contains about the same number of calories, you can see how lecithin supplementation could lead to weight gain. On the other hand, if you compensate for the lecithin by cutting more nutrient-dense foods from your diet, it could cause specific vitamin or mineral deficiencies. People taking lecithin have to choose their foods with care and may also need a one-a-day vitamin supplement containing the RDA.

Lecithin and choline chloride are found in a wide variety of foods (see Table 18), but it is difficult to ingest more than a few grams per day in this form. All the available information suggests that you need at least 20 grams to produce any significant improvement in memory, and some authorities put the figure as high as 70 grams. Improvements will be noted within about 90 minutes, and so, if nothing happens, this form of supplementation is not for you. The one other problem associated with lecithin or choline therapy is that no one has yet determined for how long a time one single dose continues to work.

The other factor that influences memory is behavior. Good sleeping habits, a balanced diet, no drug or alcohol abuse, and constant mental challenges are all ways to keep your memory in top shape. This applies to people of all ages. Just as children should be given more toys rather than fewer (several cheaper toys are better than one expensive one), challenging puzzles, and be encouraged to play with other children in order to stimulate their minds, so should we all continue to challenge our mental powers throughout our lives. By taking time out to talk to the elderly and getting them to listen to music, visit art galleries and museums and read books, we can prevent unnecessary deterioration in the mental powers of older people and even increase their IQ.

The question of which is more important, good nutrition or environmental stimulation, has long been debated. But the solution to the riddle is simple. To keep your memory and intellect in peak form, concentrate on getting both into your life.

How to Cope

To improve your memory and mental abilities:
- iron: 18 mg. for women, 10 mg. for men
- lecithin: 30 grams

OR

- choline chloride: 10 grams

CHAPTER 8

CEREBRAL ALLERGIES

Susan's friends thought she was crazy, and she often thought the same thing. Every time she had any type of cola beverage, fruit juice, or even an orange, she immediately became profoundly depressed. On one particularly horrifying occasion, after drinking several bottles of cola she had gone home in tears and attempted suicide.

It turned out that Susan wasn't crazy after all. She was suffering from what is now believed by many to be a cerebral allergy to citric acid, an ingredient found in colas and fruit juices. She did not have a mental problem, but a physical one: an allergic reaction to a particular food that affected her brain rather than her sinuses or stomach. Research in this area is still in its infancy, but many doctors now believe that the brain as well as the body may be susceptible to allergic reactions to foods, chemicals, and a host of other substances, and that such allergies may be responsible, in certain cases, for symptoms as dramatic as depression, schizophrenia, suicidal behavior, confusion, forgetfulness, hyperactivity, apathy, anxiety, slurred speech, poor concentration, and reduced muscular coordination—as well as more commonly recognized symptoms such as a runny nose or hives.

Susan was one of the lucky ones who found out about their "illness" and how it could be prevented—in her case, by avoiding all foods and beverages containing citric acid. But most people who suffer from cerebral allergies have no idea what is happening. Believing they are mentally unbalanced, they seek psychiatric help. They are generally unlikely to seek a physical cause for a mental disturbance. Some doctors— including psychiatrists and psychologists—don't even believe in cerebral allergies, although more and more research is proving their existence.*

What Is a Cerebral Allergy?

Cerebral allergies are defined as unusual brain reactions to normally innocuous substances. Those who believe that they exist say that constant exposure to common foods, environmental chemicals, and substances found naturally in the air (like pollen) can trigger a wide range of mental, emotional, and physical disorders in susceptible people. They also feel that physical and psychological stress play a role, by predisposing a person to this disorder, or by making him or her more susceptible to it. Not only such obviously "mental" disorders as hyperactivity, depression, or schizophrenia, but such "physical" ailments as asthma and ulcerative colitis are among the conditions attributed to cerebral allergies. (Remember, the mind controls the body in unexpected ways.)

One type of cerebral allergy is well understood. This is the result of the same kind of allergic response experienced by hay fever sufferers, for example. *Antigens* are foreign proteins, including bacteria and viruses. They can gain entrance into the body in a variety of ways—through the food we eat, the air we breathe, or the liquids we drink. In response, the body's natural immune system produces *antibodies* that usually break down the antigens and render them inactive. Sometimes,

---

*Their lack of belief is not entirely without reason—new discoveries are all too often taken to extremes. It is no more likely that all patients exhibiting bizarre emotional behavior are allergic, than that none are. Careful diagnosis and testing must be done to determine which is the case, or whether the behavioral problem represents a combination of both.

however, the antibody in combination with its antigen triggers the release of large quantities of a chemical called *histamine*, or other substances called *kinins* from the tissues, and the symptoms of an allergy appear.

Allergic reactions can be respiratory, such as sneezing, running nose or ears, and wheezing; gastrointestinal, such as in or around the mouth, abdominal pain, vomiting and diarrhea; dermal, such as wheals, itching, and rashes of all types; and cerebral or neurological, such as dizziness, headaches, or certain mental or emotional disturbances.

Allergic symptoms can show up in several body systems at the same time. A person with eczema (which is sometimes caused by an allergy, and can be triggered in some people by an adverse reaction to milk) may also exhibit symptoms showing a disturbance of the nervous system, including headaches and depression. On the other hand, a person with a milk allergy may have headaches and mood changes without the accompanying skin disorder, and in such cases the allergy is likely to go undiagnosed. Traditional therapies used to treat irritation of the sinuses—such as desensitizing injections or oral antihistamines—are often found also to relieve insomnia, depression, or irritability.

The Headache of Headaches

Headache is perhaps the most common symptom of a neurological allergy—specifically migraine headaches. Eight to 12 percent of all people who suffer from migraines are believed to do so because of environmental, or more commonly, food allergens.

Foods can cause migraines directly by acting as *vasodilators*. (Vasodilation is the dilation or expansion of the blood vessels.) Foods containing the substance tyramine, such as aged cheese, chocolate, canned fish, pickled herring, chicken livers, cured meats, raisins, sour cream, soy sauce, red wine, some beers, and other alcoholic beverages in general, are potent vasodilators and should be avoided if you are predisposed to migraines. The food ingredient monosodium glutamate (MSG) is thought to be responsible for what is called "Chinese Restaurant Syndrome," characterized by severe headaches.

Like migraines, cluster headaches can be caused by an allergic reaction to food, as well as by foods that act directly as vasodilators. A series of attacks that subside for a while and then strike again, cluster headaches come on suddenly without warning, and may last from several minutes to a few hours. They often strike at night, rousing the sufferer out of a sound sleep, and can be accompanied by nasal congestion and watering eyes. The pain usually affects the eyes and temples, the neck, and sometimes the shoulders. Even the upper teeth may start to ache.

Five times more men than women suffer from cluster headaches. The typical patient is a heavy smoker in his middle years with no family history of such problems (as opposed to migraines, which have a strong genetic link). If you suffer from clusters, you should stay away from vasodilators like alcohol and tyramine-containing foods, as well as the foods listed in Table 19, which have been implicated in the production of all types of headaches. If a cerebral allergy to a specific food is suspected, perform the standard elimination test yourself. First, eliminate the suspected foods from your diet, and then gradually readmit them one by one until the one(s) that triggers the headaches is discovered.

TABLE 19

Foods Commonly Found to Cause Headaches (in Susceptible People)

chocolate	garlic
cinnamon	legume (including peanuts)
corn	milk
eggs	pork
fish	wheat

Other Cerebral Allergies

When we leave the relatively clear-cut area of headaches and move to other symptoms of neurological allergy, we are entering controversial ground, despite the fact that Dr. I. S. Kahn introduced the concept of neurological hypersensitivity as long ago as 1927. In the case of allergic headaches, the most common immediate cause of the symptoms—vasodilation—is clear. However, researchers are still unsure of the possible mechanisms for other cerebral allergies. Furthermore, except in cases of the most extreme behavior, the symptoms are primarily subjective, and so difficult to define and diagnose with scientific exactitude. One can count sneezes and observe the appearance of a rash. But how can one measure degrees of hyperactivity in children or mood changes in an adult?

Perhaps the most common manifestation of a cerebral allergy is what some physicians call "tension fatigue syndrome." Symptoms may include fatigue, mental and emotional tension, irritability, pallor, circles under the eyes, a stuffy nose, headache, muscle and/or joint pains, stomach ache, and often swollen lymph glands in the neck area.

This syndrome is mainly found in children, particularly in those labeled hyperactive. It can also occur in adults, however. They lose interest in their work and/or their families, their appetite is often poor, they suffer from insomnia and complain of feeling tired all the time, find it difficult to concentrate, may experience extreme anxiety, or could exhibit compulsive behavior. They may be unrealistic about their life situation, extremely talkative, and excitable. Some of these are classic symptoms of depression, and it may be (indeed, some allergists have so stated) that among patients in mental hospitals being treated for severe depression, there are a number who are really just allergic to a particular food or inhalant.

Still, most of the cases of allergic-tension fatigue reported involve children. They may exhibit hyperactive (overactive) or underactive behavior—or alternate between the two, between a tension phase characterized by symptoms like the inability to concentrate, restlessness, drowsiness, irritability, and often aggressive behavior, and a fatigue phase in which they are listless and dull, difficult to awaken in the morning, tired all the time, and unresponsive in the classroom. Such children often have sleep disturbances, cry easily, and their movements are jerky. They are also sensitive to loud noises and bright lights.*

A Variety of Symptoms

Cerebral allergy can appear under circumstances that might normally be dismissed by the sufferer, or not linked to an allergic reaction. A mild-mannered businessperson suddenly becomes a screaming tyrant at the office after a lunch of shrimp. A normally relaxed person may become obsessive-compulsive about cleanliness, dusting shelves and tables five and six times just an hour after eating fresh strawberries.

Other types of cerebral allergies can cause symptoms that resemble alcoholic intoxication—flushing, poor coordination, confusion, reduced concentration, emotional disturbances, slurred speech, vertigo, feelings of weakness, seizures, blackouts, muscle tenderness or pain, numbness, periods of disorientation, leg or jaw spasms, vision problems, facial paralysis, stuttering and stammering, pain behind the eyeball, and inflammations of the nerves.

The agents—foods or chemicals—triggering such reactions can be very diverse and specific to each individual. A person may be susceptible to several different foods, chemicals, and substances found in the air. To complicate matters, different substances have been reported to induce the same symptoms in different people. Whereas strawberries will cause obsessive behavior in one person, eggs will have the same effect on another, but not strawberries. Finally, there is such a lack of consistency in the types of symptoms associated with cerebral allergies that many physicians continue to believe that all changes in behavior following the consumption of a food substance are purely psychosomatic, and resist the claims of "clinical ecologists" or "orthomolecular physicians" who have been able to relieve the symptoms of neurological allergy and restore normal feelings and behavior by control-

---

*Although the more radical allergists maintain that all such children have an allergy, most are less certain. In fact, teachers, parents, as well as physicians, have differing views on what degree of activity constitutes hyperactivity.

ling a person's exposure to offending inhalants and by eliminating certain foods from the diet.

The effects of all potentially toxic substances acting on a person are thought to be additive. The total problem would therefore be caused not only by foods, but also by chemical substances in the environment combined with the food, as well as by other predisposing factors—such as heat or cold, altitude, exercise, age, smoking, and stress. Susan, the girl described at the beginning of this chapter who is sensitive to citric acid, might not be affected after drinking a glass of Coke or orange juice while sitting in the comfort of her own home, but might become severely depressed after drinking the same beverage at a stressful time.

Clinical ecologists theorize that the more frequently a person eats an allergy-producing substance, the greater the chance that he or she will develop a cerebral allergy to it. However, they also suggest that once the allergy has developed, the symptoms will becomes less severe the more the person is exposed to the offending substance, although they will never disappear entirely unless the substance is avoided completely.

Why Does a Cerebral Allergy Occur?

Allergists offer several theories on the mechanisms that may lead to cerebral allergic reactions. It is thought that some patients' bodies produce too few antibodies to effectively negate given antigens. Allergists have also hypothesized that the compounds formed when the antibodies and antigens combine damage the blood-brain barrier, and this is what causes the behavioral changes.

Dr. Michael Russell of the Behavior Research Center at the University of California at San Francisco has come up with another theory, having to do with the well-known story of Pavlov's dog. As we know, Pavlov rang a bell every day just before feeding his dog. The dog become conditioned to salivate every time he heard the bell, in anticipation of eating food—whether or not a meal was provided afterward. Dr. Russell believes that some forms of cerebral allergy are acquired in the same way. A young child who develops an allergy to eggs may also develop allergic symptoms whenever he or she sees or smells eggs, or even encounters, (by sight or smell or sound) anything associated with the eating of eggs—such as dishwashing liquid, the formica on the kitchen table where he or she first ate eggs, the smell of spices sometimes used in egg dishes, or even the sounds of a food mixer.

Dr. Russell has proven his point in animal studies. A rabbit, artificially made allergic to egg protein and exposed to the smell of garlic at the same time showed allergic symptoms not only when fed eggs, but also when it came near garlic. Russell believes that associated experiences trigger the brain to set the immune system in motion. The net result is an allergic reaction.

It is likely that both immune and nonimmune factors combine to produce the symptoms in question. The kinins released into the body's tissues in response to the complexes formed by the combination of antibody and antigen can alter the sensitivity of brain cells to acetylcholine, serotonin, dopamine, and norepinephrine and have been shown to alter behavior. There are also some data that show that hormones produced in the intestines, such as cholecystokinin (which helps to control appetite and is involved in digestion) may be released in abnormally high quantities by certain food substances and subsequently enter the brain via the bloodstream and affect brain function.

Specific Foods and Behavior

Although it has been hypothesized that particular foods can cause or aggravate specific psychiatric symptoms, little conclusive research has yet been done. As we mentioned, citric acid has been linked to depression. Another area of research connects sugar and hyperactivity. It has been shown that in hyperactive six-year-olds the greater the amount of sugar in the foods they eat, the greater their restlessness and the more frequent their episodes of destructive-aggressive behavior; this is true if the sugar is taken in a concentrated form, without being balanced with protein and fat. Red Dye #3, found in many commercially prepared foods and in drugs and cosmetics, has also been implicated as a cause of or contributing factor to hyperactivity. Finally, there is evidence of a link between milk and/or gluten (a protein mostly found in wheat and some other grains) and schizophrenia, including reports of the rapid improvement of schizophrenics who received a milk-free, gluten-free diet.

Diagnosing Cerebral Allergies

The most popularly used test for diagnosing cerebral allergies is the "challenge test." Here, the relevant substance is avoided for four days in order to eliminate any adaptations the body may have made to the substance and thus to leave the person once more susceptible to a severe reaction when again exposed five to 12 days later. It is important that reexposure occur within this time frame, since after more than two weeks of avoidance frequent exposure is needed before symptoms develop, comes into play, and any reaction to the reexposure may therefore escape detection.

A second approach is the "rotary diversified diet," in which none of the suspect foods is eaten more often than once in four days so that the possible culprits are rotated, and in this way, pinpointed. The food most often found to be guilty of producing a wide range of symptoms in different people are:

- chocolate
- cola beverages
- eggs
- fruits or fruit juices containing citric acid
- milk
- spices and seasonings
- wheat

There are other tests that can be done, but they are not considered by most to be scientifically valid. "Cytotoxic" testing is a procedure in which white blood cells taken from the patient are mixed with food extracts. If the cells show subtle changes in shape or size in response to a particular extract, the person is said to be allergic to that food. However, the results of this type of test often do not agree with the person's response to the actual foods in a challenge test. Hence, cytotoxic testing is considered virtually useless by the American Academy of Allergy and Immunology.

Another controversial diagnostic technique is "intradermal neutralization." Here, very dilute extracts of food substances are injected into the skin (usually, a series of these dilutions is prepared and tested at one time). Some will cause symptoms and others will not. Unfortunately, the symptoms exhibited are often so much weaker that those produced from a challenge test that the intradermal method is not considered reliable.

In Conclusion

The treatment for cerebral allergies is dependent on controlling your exposure to environmental inhalants and eliminating from the diet whatever food substances cause the problem. Antihistamines may be helpful in relieving some of the symptoms. Very often the problem can be traced to common foods—especially milk, cola, citrus fruits and beverages, wheat, eggs, chocolate, and spices and seasonings.

Although we must not explain away all types of abnormal emotional behavior as allergies to certain foods or other substances, the possibility that an allergy may be the cause of or exacerbate conditions like hyperactivity in children and mental disturbances in adults must not be overlooked.

CHAPTER 9

BURNING THE BRAIN
The Effects of Tobacco, Caffeine, and Alcohol

Alcohol, caffeine-containing foods and beverages, and cigarettes are all integral parts of our society. If used in moderation, none of these three "habits" is harmful to the brain or, with the exception of cigarette smoking, dangerous to overall health. However, in excess all three substances can injure the mind and body.

Tobacco

By now, everyone, is aware of the physical dangers of cigarette smoking. The life of a 25-year-old smoking two packs a day is shortened by 8.3 years. Lung cancer, heart disease, and emphysema are all either helped along or directly caused by the use of tobacco. Still, millions of people continue to smoke despite all the warnings. They crave cigarettes, find it "impossible" to stop smoking, and even cut financial corners so they can afford to feed their habit.

The level of nicotine present in the brain is crucial to a smoker's behavior. The actions of chronic, heavy smokers suggest that they adjust the concentration of nicotine in their brains within a very narrow range that gives them the satisfaction they need. For example, when they smoke stronger cigarettes, they smoke fewer; when lighter cigarettes are all there is around, they smoke more. Although smokers who switch to low tar and nicotine cigarettes tend to reduce their nicotine intake, they offset the potential benefit by the greater amount of smoke they inhale with its inherent toxic gases including hydrogen cyanide, nitrogen oxide, ammonia, and carbon monoxide. It has a stronger affinity by 200 times for red blood cells than does oxygen. Since red blood cells carry oxygen throughout the body, the carbon monoxide is replacing the oxygen and depleting the body and brain's supply. Carbon monoxide also acts directly on the brain to impair vision, hearing, and judgment.

Nicotine reaches the brain within eight seconds of a smoker's inhalation. Within ten to fifteen minutes after finishing the cigarette, the level of nicotine declines rapidly as it is absorbed by other tissues and organs of the body. Then another cigarette is needed in order to raise brain nicotine levels to the point where the smoker feels satisfied. Nicotine increases brain levels of norepinephrine and dopamine and increases the electrical activity of the brain. This seems to facilitate memory and makes the smoker more alert and less irritable. It also stimulates brain centers concerned with respiration, blood pressure, and pleasure (i.e., the hypothalamus), decreases the appetite, and relaxes the muscles (but, oddly enough, makes the hands less steady).

Nicotine tolerance definitely increases with use. When a person first starts smoking, he may feel nauseated and dizzy. However, if he persists, he will start to feel a "lift" and lose the ill side effects first experienced. Usage can then increase from five to 10 cigarettes a day and rapidly climb to the one- to two-pack-a-day category.

Regular smokers experience withdrawal symptoms from one to two hours after their last cigarette. The usual symptoms (in addition to the craving for nicotine, which subsides after a maximum of a few weeks) are irritability, anxiety, restlessness, poor concentration, and reduced pulse rate and blood pressure. Drowsiness, headaches, increased appetite, insomnia, diarrhea, and constipation may also occur. Some smokers complain that the increased appetite and inability to concentrate persists for weeks or months, but the other symptoms do subside within a shorter period of time, which differs from smoker to smoker.

Nicotine is in the same chemical family as strychnine, quinine, mescaline, heroin, and morphine. Actually, nicotine addiction is established more quickly and is often harder to kick then heroin addiction—in fact, many doctors feel that it is one of the most powerful addictions a person can have. The brain gets used to its supply of nicotine, which is hardly surprising, considering the fact that it gets heavy daily reinforcement from a regular smoker. If you smoke one pack a day for a year, your brain will receive 50,000 doses of nicotine. And cigarette smokers, unlike people who use stronger drugs, are seldom occasional indulgers. People may drink wine only once in a while, or take a sleeping pill from time to time, but most smokers are at it all day, every day.

As far as nutrient interaction, the news for smokers isn't good. Smoking depletes the body of vitamins C, B_6, and B_{12} (actually, it is the cyanide present in cigarettes that robs the body of B_{12}). It might be wise for smokers to take a daily 500 mg. supplement of vitamin C, since the brain needs this nutrient for many functions, including the manufacture of neurotransmitters. B_{12} protects the body against anemia, as well as keeping brain myelin in healthy working order. Although nonvegetarians seldom need supplements of B_{12} even if they are heavy smokers, vegetarians who smoke should take a 6 mcg. per day supplement, unless they eat foods especially containing this nutrient. Vitamin B_6, necessary for general brain metabolism, should be supplemented by 2-3 mg. per day.

During pregnancy, cigarette smoking deprives the fetus of nutrients due to the constriction of blood vessels caused by the nicotine and the reduction in the oxygen supply caused by the carbon monoxide. Infants born to mothers who are heavy smokers weigh on average six ounces less than those born to nonsmokers, and they are more irritable, show impaired learning abilities, a reduced interest in their surroundings, a three-month delay in the acquisition of reading skills, and a five-month delay in the acquisition of mathematical skills. Some of these effects are long term—some children are smaller and still have impaired reading abilities at age seven. It is easy to see why pregnant women should not smoke.

As far as brain and body health is concerned, smoking tobacco is not a good idea.

Caffeine

The stimulant known as caffeine—found in coffee, tea, cola drinks, and chocolate—has been the subject of much recent controversy. Consequently, the sales of decaffeinated coffees, herbal teas, and caffeine-free colas have risen dramatically. But caffeine is also found in many other products, such as cold remedies, cough medicines, and "wake-up" pills, which are all distributed over the counter.

Caffeine is a minor stimulant that reduces fatigue and increases the feeling of alertness. Actually, caffeine, its cousin theobromide, and the methylxanthines, the larger grouping of

TABLE 20

Dietary Sources of Caffeine (mg)

Coffee:
Drip (5 fl. oz.)	110 -164
Percolated (5 fl. oz.)	93 -134
Instant (5 fl.oz.)	50 - 65
Decaffeinated (5 fl. oz.)	2 - 5

Tea:
One-minute brew (5 fl. oz.)	9 - 33
Three-minute brew (5 fl. oz.)	20 - 40
Five-minute brew (5 fl. oz.)	20 - 50
Canned iced tea (12 fl. oz.)	22 - 36

Cocoa and Chocolate:
Cocoa beverage (6 fl. oz.)	2 - 8
Milk chocolate (1 oz.)	1 - 15
Baking chocolate (1 oz.)	25 - 35

Cola drinks (12 fl. oz.)   35 - 45

chemicals these two substances belong to, had a glorious past. The Aztecs and ancient Arabic cultures considered foods containing this chemical "gifts from the Gods." They respected the stimulating effects of these substances and used them to increase their energy as well as in their religious rites.

Today we must take a dimmer view, without overreacting. Within five minutes of drinking a cup of coffee, you feel less drowsy, less fatigued, and have a more rapid and clear flow of thought. Caffeine enables you to keep up a sustained intellectual effort for a longer period of time and decreases your reaction time to unpredictable events, such as making an emergency stop in a car. However, tasks involving delicate muscular coordination (like painting a picture) and/or accurate timing (like timing a race with a stop watch), or arithmetic skills, may be impaired. The effect of caffeine peaks in about 30 minutes and then continues to sustain its effect in the same way for the next eight hours—the time taken for the body fully to metabolize the caffeine. Eighty percent is excreted through the urine during this time. Women who take oral contraceptives and pregnant women in the last half of their pregnancy take twice as long to metabolize caffeine. On the other hand, cigarette smoking speeds up caffeine metabolism.

People's reactions to caffeine vary, but in general, between 85 and 250 mg. of caffeine (one to three cups of coffee) should improve most people's performance. Anything over that amount can cause nervousness, restlessness, irritability, tingling in the fingers and toes, and insomnia. Drinking a beverage that contains caffeine before bedtime usually delays sleep, shortens sleeping time, reduces the average depth of sleep, and reduces the amount of dream (REM) sleep. Some people are very susceptible to the effects of caffeine and show these adverse reactions after drinking only one cup of coffee, whereas others may be able to drink as many as six cups of strong coffee before they show any side effects.

For most people, the regular consumption of about 350 mg. per day causes physical dependence. If the intake is interrupted, withdrawal symptoms can be experienced, headaches being the most common. The sudden absence of caffeine makes regular users feel irritable, tired, nauseated, nervous, and unable to concentrate. These symptoms may last anywhere from a few days to a few weeks. It is best to gradually eliminate caffeine from your diet.

Excessive intake of caffeine—over 600 mg. per day, or eight cups of coffee—can be toxic and lead to chronic insomnia, persistent anxiety, paranoia, depression, stomach upset, and frequent urination. Nobody is sure what caffeine does to the brain. Current opinion favors the theory that it interferes with the normal action of a brain chemical adenosine, which is a natural tranquilizer. This leads to overstimulation of the brain. Although caffeine or xanthines in general have never been found to cause permanent brain damage, some studies have suggested that they may aggravate hyperactivity in susceptible children.

During pregnancy, large doses of caffeine (eight or more cups of coffee per day) can lead to impaired fetal growth and abnormal behavior in the infant, although the results are still inconclusive. Nevertheless, pregnant women should cut down on their consumption of caffeine.

Caffeine impairs the body's absorption of dietary iron and can lead to iron deficiency, particularly in people who tend to have a poor iron status—such as premenopausal women (especially those who menstruate heavily), the elderly, teenagers, children, and vegetarians. Foods rich in iron should be included in the diet to prevent a deficiency—red meats, fish, poultry, peas, raisins, soybean curd, and dried apricots.* Iron is of course needed for the manufacture of red blood cells, which maintain the oxygen-carrying capacity of the blood. It is also an integral part of many enzymes in the brain, including some that break down nutrients to supply the brain with energy and others that are involved in the manufacture of neurotransmitters.

Caffeine is not at all dangerous when consumed in small to moderate quantities and may even be helpful at times to improve work performance. However, excessive use is no longer advised as it not only has a destructive effect on the brain but may also be a causative agent of some types of cancer and of hardening of the arteries.

---

*For a complete list of iron-rich foods, see Table 17, p. 92.

Alcohol

After tobacco and caffeine, alcohol is the most freely abused drug in our society. Casual and social drinking—from indulging at lunch or at a party to taking a drink or two to calm the nerves—have become a part of everyday life. While approximately two-thirds of all adults drink alcoholic beverages, we normally regard it as a problem only when a person becomes a chronic heavy drinker, an "alcoholic." Unfortunately, there is cause for real concern even when a person drinks moderately. Apart from alcohol's numerous toxic effects on the body's major organs, it also disrupts and diminishes the smooth operation of motor and thought processes in the brain.

Absorption and Metabolism

Alcohol is very rapidly absorbed into the body. On an empty stomach, 85 percent of the alcohol you drink is fully absorbed through the walls of the stomach and small intestine into the bloodstream within 20 minutes. Watery drinks, like beer, are absorbed more slowly. Foods, especially fatty foods, delay absorption because they slow down the emptying of the stomach into the small intestine, where the alcohol is absorbed quickest. Carbonated beverages, on the other hand, speed up the emptying of the stomach. Other factors that can affect absorption include your emotional and/or physical state and your body chemistry—if you are tired, under a lot of stress, depressed, or nervous, you will absorb alcohol more rapidly. As you age, you are better able to tolerate the alcohol you drink.

Alcohol passes from the bloodstream into every part of the body except bone, including the brain. Only about 5 percent is eliminated from the body via breath, urine, or sweat. The rest is broken down by the liver—it processes alcohol at about one-third of a fluid ounce per hour, less than what is contained in an ounce of whiskey. The unprocessed alcohol continues to circulate through the blood. This means that what you take in from two cocktails, each about 1-1/2 fluid ounces, consumed one hour before dinner, is still in your body three to four hours later, although in ever-diminishing amounts.

It is because the liver breaks down alcohol at this fixed rate that trying to sober someone up by giving him black coffee or throwing him under a cold shower is useless. Caffeine does not speed up the degradation of alcohol in the body—all it produces is a wide-awake drunk who may be deluded into thinking he can drive home. The chronic use of alcohol does result in an increased capacity to metabolize it more rapidly and does enable chronic drinkers to function with a much higher level of it in their blood. However, if you stop drinking for a few weeks, the increased capacities to degrade alcohol and to perform under its influence are gone.

Effects on the Brain

Although many of us tend to think of the effects of alcohol as stimulating, in reality alcohol depresses brain activity. The feeling of stimulation it gives results from the unrestrained activity of various parts of the brain as a result of the depression of the inhibitory control mechanisms. Alcohol exerts its effects first on the most complicated actions of the brain—the first mental processes to be affected are those which depend on training and previous experience, and that make for self-restraint and sobriety. Memory, concentration, and insight are dulled and then lost. As inhibitions are released, you normally become friendlier, more gregarious, and expansive. You may lose your sexual inhibitions. However, although sex drive is increased, performance is impaired. Even Shakespeare commented on this effect in Macbeth:

> Macduff: What three things does drink especially provoke?
> Porter: Marry, Sir, nose-painting, sleep, and urine. Lechery, Sir, it provokes, and unprovokes: it provokes the desire, but it takes away the performance.

With increased alcohol consumption some drinkers suffer from uncontrollable mood swings and frequent emotional outbursts. These mental changes are accompanied by impaired motor ability (including muscle function, reaction time, eyesight, depth perception, and night vision). Even moderate amounts of alcohol—one or two glasses—produce enough impairment to seriously affect a person's ability to drive.

As the blood levels of alcohol rise, a sedative effect increases, which calms and tranquilizes. This gives way to an anesthetic effect that numbs, and finally a hypnotic effect, which causes sleep. If an enormous amount of alcohol is taken, it can even cause death, by slowing the breathing to a point where it stops altogether.

Table 21 shows how different quantities of alcohol can affect behavior over a specific time period:

People who drink four or more drinks of hard liquor or its equivalent a day suffer from the death of cells from just about every structure of the brain. This neuronal death is proportionate to the amount of alcohol consumed. Chronic alcohol use also changes the actual structure of the membranes surrounding the brain cells and the blood-brain barrier. The former affects neurotransmission, the latter the flow of substances to and from the brain. Any amount of alcohol can affect the relative levels of the different neurotransmitters, and chronic use can permanently disrupt this delicate balance. This is why people who drink heavily throughout their lives begin to show impaired mental performance and exhibit bizarre behavior that can no longer be corrected by the cessation of drinking.

TABLE 21

The Effects of Alcohol

Quantity of Whiskey Consumed Over Two Hours	Result
2 fl. oz.	euphoria, minor movement disturbances
2.4 fl. oz.	problems with vision
3 fl. oz.	impaired driving ability
4-6 fl. oz.	complete lack of coordination
8-12 fl. oz.	loss of memory
12-14 fl. oz.	coma
14-16 fl. oz.	possible death

Nutrition, Alcohol, and the Brain

Chronic drinking also leads to nutrient deficiencies that exacerbate the effects of the alcohol on the brain and cause additional behavioral and functional abnormalities. This can happen in one of two ways. First, heavy drinkers would often have a "liquid meal" instead of eating regular food. As alcohol contains seven calories per gram and little else in the way of nutrients, this can lead to serious nutritional deficiencies. In fact, heavy drinkers rarely eat normal, balanced meals, and full-fledged alcoholics often suffer from extreme deficiencies. Heavy drinkers can easily consume 1,800 calories a day in the form of alcohol alone! That doesn't leave much room for food. What makes the situation worse is the second fact—that alcohol impairs the absorption and metabolism of many nutrients, including amino acids, vitamins B_1, B_2, B_6, A, and D, folic acid, calcium, magnesium, zinc and glucose, all of which have key roles in brain function (see Chapter 2).

Heavy drinkers are especially deficient in thiamine (vitamin B_1) and magnesium. Alcohol decreases the absorption of thiamine and increases the excretion of magnesium. Both are needed by the body for carbohydrate metabolism and carbohydrate is, as you know by now, the brain's main fuel source. Deficiency of thiamine leads to Wernicke Korsakoff's syndrome—amnesia, loss of short-term memory, disorientation, hallucination, emotional outbursts, double vision, depression, anxiety, aggressive behavior, and loss of muscle control. A lack of magnesium exacerbates all these symptoms. If you drink two or more drinks a day you should take a supplement containing the RDA for the vitamins affected by alcohol consumption, along with calcium and 300 mg. of magnesium.

Heavy drinkers can also cause a weight problem or make an existing one much worse. If you consume 1,800 calories a day in the form of alcohol and also eat a regular diet the extra calories will be laid down as fat tissue. At this rate of consumption you could gain three to four pounds a week.

Alcohol and Women

Women absorb alcohol more easily during the premenstrual stage, although the high estrogen levels at this time seem to reduce the behavioral effects of the drug. Alcohol consumption during pregnancy is not advised. Alcohol, especially during the first three months of pregnancy, can lead to a condition called fetal alcohol syndrome, which causes fetal abnormalities including brain damage, mental retardation, deformities of the limbs, joints, fingers, face, and heart, cleft palate, and poor coordination. Sometimes fetal alcohol syndrome does not show up until adolescence when it may appear for the first time as hyperactivity and learning and perceptual problems. No one knows how much alcohol is safe. Six or more drinks a day or occasional binge drinking is definitely harmful, but even one or two drinks may be too much. To be on the safe side you should avoid alcohol entirely if you are pregnant or trying to conceive. As alcohol also gets into breast-milk it is best to avoid alcohol when you are breast-feeding. There is no truth to the old wive's tale that alcohol helps the milk flow more freely. In fact it inhibits milk flow.

Combating a Hangover

For many people, one of the most unpleasant aspects of drinking is the morning after. Even for light drinkers, the collection of symptoms known as a hangover can be a devastating physical experience. It can include headache, confusion, nausea, vomiting, fatigue, anxiety, and gastrointestinal disorders. Some of these symptoms can be eased by eating the right foods.

● Headaches: These are caused by the alcohol's dilation of the blood vessels in the head. Coffee is the best remedy for this, as caffeine is a vaso-constrictor. So is aspirin. For some people, hot showers also seem to help.

● Nausea and gastric distress: Coffee and aspirin (if not buffered) should be avoided, as they tend to irritate the digestive tract. Toast, soft-boiled eggs, and other bland foods are the best bet.

● Thirst or bloating: Slightly salty liquids, like good old chicken soup, work wonders.

● Muscle aches or general fatigue: Coffee and a hot shower are suggested.

117

- Dizziness and weakness caused by low blood sugar: Drinking orange juice is one good way to boost these depleted levels.

Withdrawal

Alcoholics suffer from serious symptoms when they stop drinking. The chronic maintenance of high concentrations of alcohol in their blood causes a state of physical dependence. Withdrawal symptoms most commonly appear within 12 to 72 hours after the last drink. However, even a relative decline in blood concentrations—a reduction in the total daily intake or a change in the pattern of drinking—cause the same symptoms.

With a low level of dependence withdrawal may amount to disturbed sleep, nausea, weakness, anxiety, and mild tremors that last for less than a day. When the dependence is severe, the symptoms can be life-threatening. They include insomnia, visual and auditory hallucinations, disorientation, convulsions, epileptic seizures, severe shaking, acute anxiety and fear, agitation, increased heart rate, fever and excessive sweating, all of which can last for five to seven days. A high-carbohydrate diet seems to help alcoholics through this period. It is believed that the powerful effect produced in the pleasure centers of the brain by the sweet foods offsets the desire for alcohol.

Recently detoxicated alcoholics perform more poorly in learning tasks, especially those involving short-term memory. Partial recovery is possible with prolonged abstinence, but complete restoration to normal is unlikely if the person has been an alcoholic for several years.

Is Alcoholism Inherited?

Alcoholism as a disease does seem to run in families, and statistical studies have shown that people who have alcoholics in their immediate families run a four times greater risk of contracting the same problem than do the offspring of nondrinkers. The pattern of electrical activity in the brain of offspring of many alcoholics shows differences that suggest genetic influences on the development of the disease.

In Conclusion

Alcohol is not all bad. In small amounts, if used infrequently, it can be quite pleasant. It can stimulate the appetite, reduce tensions and anxieties, and facilitate conversation. In large amounts, however, it causes a complete lack of inhibition, impaired motor coordination, irresponsible behavior, gastro-intestinal disturbances, cirrhosis of the liver, pancreatitis, memory loss, intellectual impairment, and a whole host of other related mental and physical ailments.

Smoking is never good for your health. Caffeine, in small or moderate amounts can be fine. And any nutritional deficiencies caused by these habits should be corrected by supplementation.

How to Cope

If you smoke:
- Vitamin C   500 mg. supplement daily
- Vitamin B_6 2-3 mg. supplement daily
- Vitamin B_{12} 6 mcg. supplement daily (for vegetarians)

If you use caffeine:
- Iron   From red meat, fish, poultry, peas, raisins, soybean curd, dried apricots

If you drink:
- Vitamin A   4,000-5,000 I.U. supplement daily
- Vitamin B_1 1.5 mg. supplement daily
- Vitamin B_2 1.7 mg. supplement daily
- Vitamin B_6 2-3 mg. supplement daily
- Vitamin D   400 I.U. supplement daily
- Folic acid   400 mcg. supplement daily
- Calcium   1,000 mg. supplement daily
- Zinc   15 mg. supplement daily
- Glucose   110 gm. as food daily
- Magnesium   300-350 mg. supplement daily

CHAPTER 10

Nutrition for the Growing Brain

The human brain begins growing in the womb and the majority of this development does not slow down until the age of six. Growth in the brain of the fetus, infant, and young child is time-dependent. This means that the brain grows in specific stages at specific times. If it does not have all the nutrients essential for its growth at those times, damage or malformation can result, and it cannot be corrected at a later date. A developing infant who is fed poorly during its period of brain growth may be left with permanent learning disabilities, no matter what is done at a later date to correct the nutritional deficiency.

Malnutrition is potentially most damaging to the fetus or infant when the brain cells are growing in number. It can cause a reduction in the number of brain cells the child possesses, as well as the size of his or her brain. When malnutrition occurs at a later stage in brain development, fewer dendrites are made, along with less myelin. The production of neurotransmitters and the development of the child's ability to respond to outside stimuli—sights and sounds—may also be impaired.

As you can see, the right nutritional program is never more

important to a human's mental capabilities than during the period of brain growth.

Critical Periods of Cellular Growth

Fetal life is a time of tremendous cellular development in the brain. While in the womb, the brain grows until it is the largest organ of the fetus's body. By the fifth month, it is almost the same size as the trunk. This early growth spurt of the brain's cells is due to cell multiplication rather than cell enlargement.

Cell division or multiplication occurs at different times in different areas of the brain, and at different rates (although there is some overlap). Also, division in the two types of brain cells-neurons and glial cells—occurs at different times, again with some overlap. Neuronal division precedes that of the glial cells.

The two hemispheres of the forebrain are the first to go through a spurt of neuron proliferation. This happens during the third and fourth months of pregnancy, and peaks at 26 weeks. During this stage of growth it has been estimated that neurons are being created at the rate of 250,000 per minute. However, most of the neurons are formed during the second three months of pregnancy, and at birth, the baby's one-pound brain contains an estimated 100 billion neurons, virtually the full amount found in the three-pound adult brain.

The glial cells are also rapidly forming while the child is in the womb. During the fifth month of pregnancy, they begin their growth spurt. This glial cell division peaks at birth and begins to decline during the third month after birth, although it continues at a reduced rate of growth until the child is two to three years old.

Behavioral Development

What does this all mean in terms of the baby's behavior? By the tenth week of pregnancy, electrical activity can be detected in certain areas of the brain, particularly the areas that coordinate sleeping and waking. By the 12th to 16th week the face and hands can move, directed by the brain. By two and a half months, the fetus is swallowing amniotic fluid. By seven and a half months the nervous system has advanced to the point where the fetus can open its eyes and raise its hands to its mouth and suck on them. At birth, the infant can breathe, see, and move of its own volition. During this initial period after birth, however, it can do little more than cry, suck, excrete, and sleep.

Various brain centers, including parts of the hypothalamus, are believed to be involved in regulating the newborn child's eating cycles. Although at first the child will eat every four hours, by six months of age it begins to follow a more regular eating pattern, sleeping more at night and eating mostly during the day.

The Fetus and the Brain

Malnutrition During Pregnancy

A mother who does not eat properly during pregnancy can seriously endanger her child's physical and mental health. Malnutrition at this time can retard the rate of fetal cell division, resulting in a permanent reduction in the number of brain cells. The brain needs nutrients to grow. Severe malnutrition affects mainly the neurons; malnutrition during the early postnatal period affects mainly the glial cells. In either case, the child can be left with too little basic machinery in its brain to function normally.

During pregnancy, both gross malnutrition caused by the intake of too little food, as well as subtle deficiencies of a specific vitamin (like folic acid) or mineral (like zinc) have been linked to brain growth retardation.

If the mother suffers from a particular nutrient deficiency for a short period of time, after which the missing nutrient is provided, the rate of cell multiplication in the fetus's brain will increase again, but not always in a normal pattern. Because of the complex programming of brain growth and development, interference with one step may not be reversible once its "time" has passed. This, in turn, can interfere will all the subsequent stages of growth, which were dependent on the first one. The domino theory applies. If one section of the brain is affected by malnutrition when it is growing, it can disturb the whole chain of events. This interdependence of developmental processes in the central nervous system complicates any attempt to repair nutritional damage—more so than in any other part of the body.

Therefore, the earlier the period of growth retardation, the more serious the subsequent developmental problems will be. Infants who suffer from growth retardation at a point earlier than the 24th to 26th week of gestation are more seriously affected than those who suffer from it later on. It is essential, then, for a woman to be in good nutritional status throughout her pregnancy.

Protein and Energy Deficiency

Studies have suggested that if a pregnant woman does not take in enough calories and protein in the beginning, the rapid brain cell multiplication occurring at this time will be in-

---

TABLE 22

Good Food Sources of Protein
(Each portion provides approximately 20 g. of protein)

FOOD	AMOUNT (ounces)
baked beans	1 1/2
beef, cooked, lean or fat	3
beef, ground, cooked	3
beef, sirloin steak, cooked, lean or fat	3
calf's liver, fried	3
cheese, blue	3
cheese, Cheddar	3
cheese, cottage	2/3 cup
chicken, cooked	2
eggs, 3	4
lamb chop, cooked	3
lentils, cooked	1 1/4 cups
milk, full-cream or skimmed	2 1/2 cups
pork, loin, cooked	3
peanuts, roasted	3
salmon, cooked	3
shrimp, cooked	3
sunflower seeds	3
tuna, tinned in oil, drained	3
veal cutlet, cooked	3
yogurt, low fat, fruit-flavored	16

---

terrupted. This results in a smaller newborn head size and a smaller brain in proportion to the body size. Although brain size alone is not an indication of intelligence or normality, a lot of evidence shows that an undersized brain often does mean lowered intellect and diminished brain functions.

Energy Needs During Pregnancy

Women should take in 300 to 400 calories extra each day during pregnancy, to meet the added demands of the fetus for energy. Women who are very active, or who exercise, should consume a little more than this. Since most of us do not count our calories every day, the best way to see if you are eating enough is to watch how much weight you gain. The correct weight gain is from 22 to 28 pounds. If you were underweight before pregnancy, you should gain this amount *plus* the weight you need to put you back to normal. If you are over-weight, you still need to gain at least 16 pounds.

Protein Needs During Pregnancy

Protein intake should increase from 44 to 74 grams a day. This means adding generous portions of protein-rich foods to the diet, including beef, fish, poultry, cheese, and nuts.

Vegetarians must combine foods to improve the nutrient-giving quality of vegetable proteins. The protein quality of beans and rice, for instance, increases by 43% when the two are eaten together. In general, grains should be combined with legumes (peas, beans, lentils); nuts and seeds with vegetables. The nutritional value of all vegetables foods can be increased by combining them with eggs and milk.

Vitamins and Minerals

Subtle nutritional imbalances can have significant effects on the growing brain. This is why pregnant women should make sure that they eat a well-balanced diet at all times. Unfortunately, in all ages and economic groups, the dietary histories of most women show inadequate intakes of:

● calcium, needed for the normal activity of neurons

● Iron, needed for energy, for maintaining the proper oxygen-carrying capacity of the blood, and for making neurotransmitters and DNA

● vitamin A, needed for protein and DNA manufacture folic

acid, needed to help the brain make proteins, fats, DNA, RNA, and acetylcholine
- vitamin C, needed to help the brain use protein
- B-complex, needed for the manufacture of cells, myelin, and neurotransmitters
- zinc, for energy, DNA, RNA, and protein manufacture
- copper, for energy and myelin manufacture

Body stores of vitamin B_6 and folic acid may have been depleted before pregnancy if the woman was taking oral contraceptives or had an intrauterine device (IUD), which can

TABLE 23

Good Food Sources of Iron

FOOD	SERVING SIZE	IRON (mg)
Amaranth	3 1/2 ounces	2.0 - 4.0
Apricots, dried	6 large halves	1.5 - 2.0
Barley	1/2 cup	1.5 - 2.0
Beans, green	1 cup	1.5 - 2.0
Beans, cooked	1/2 cup	2.0 - 4.0
Beef, lean	3 ounces	4.0 - 5.0
Berries	1 cup	0.7 - 1.4
Bologna	3 to 4 ounces	1.5 - 2.0
Bread	1 slice	0.3 - 0.7
Brewer's yeast	1 tablespoon	1.5 - 2.0
Broccoli	1 cup	0.7 - 1.4
Buckwheat	1/2 cup	1.5 - 2.0
Bulgur wheat, dry	2 tablespoons	0.7 - 1.4
Carrots	1 cup	0.7 - 1.4
Chicken, all cuts	3 to 4 ounces	1.5 - 2.0
Collards	1 cup	0.7 - 1.4
Corn grits	1 cup	0.3 - 0.7
Cream of wheat	1 cup	0.7 - 1.4
Eggplant	1/2 cup	0.3 - 0.7
Figs, dried	3 medium	2.0 - 4.0
Fruits, including apples, bananas, cherries, melons, citrus, pineapple, etc.	1 piece	0.3 - 0.7

aggravate deficiencies by increasing menstrual blood flow.

A woman should be in excellent nutritional health even before she becomes pregnant. Although there is still some debate over whether or not women should regularly take vitamin and mineral supplements, the benefits seem to far outweigh the risks, especially if a woman is not getting enough calcium, zinc, iron, or folic acid in her diet. However, these supplements should not be taken in megadose amounts. More than 100,000 IUs of vitamin A taken every day for several weeks can cause serious fetal malformation. More than 1,000 IUs of vitamin D taken every day results in excessively high

TABLE 23 (Continued)

FOOD	SERVING SIZE	IRON (mg)
Ham	2 ounces	1.5 - 2.0
Lamb, lean	4 ounces	4.0 - 5.0
Liver, calf's	1 ounce	4.0 - 5.0
Molasses, blackstrap	1 tablespoon	2.0 - 4.0
Mushrooms	1/3 cup	0.3 - 0.7
Oatmeal	1 cup	1.5 - 2.0
Pasta	1/2 cup	0.3 - 0.7
Peanut butter	2 tablespoons	0.3 - 0.7
Peas, cooked	1/2 cup	2.0 - 4.0
Popcorn (popped)	1 cup	0.3 - 0.7
Potato	1 medium	0.7 - 1.4
Pumpkin seeds	1 to 2 tablespoons	0.7 - 1.4
Raisins	1/2 cup	4.0 - 5.0
Rice, cooked white or brown	1 cup	0.7 - 1.4
Tomato	1 small	0.3 - 0.7
Soybean curd	4 ounces	2.0 - 4.0
Tortilla	6 - inch diameter	0.7 - 1.4
Wheatena	2/3 cup	0.7 - 1.4

blood calcium levels, which have been linked to mental retardation in the infant.

Iron

Infants who are born to iron-deficient mothers have low stores of iron from the start. Iron deficiency can lead to serious brain dysfunctions, since iron is involved in all cell multiplication and growth, as well as influencing the oxygen-carrying capacity of the blood. Pregnant women must conscientiously meet their iron needs daily. They should take 60 mg. of iron a day, over and above the 18 mg. normally needed. The foods listed in Table 23 are rich in iron and should be added to the diet on a regular basis during pregnancy. Red meat provides the most efficiently absorbed form of iron.

It is very difficult to get all the iron one needs during pregnancy simply by eating iron-rich foods. Therefore, a pregnant woman should take an oral supplement of 30-60 mg. of ferrous sulfate daily (the most easily-absorbed supplemental form). It is best to take this supplement with food, as it can upset the stomach when taken on its own.

Zinc

Studies done on rhesus monkeys have shown the importance of zinc to the maternal diet. Normal young rhesus monkeys play freely and exuberantly. But if during pregnancy females are fed a diet deficient in zinc, their infants will act withdrawn, play less with others, and cling more to their mothers. By ten months of age, the infants whose mothers were zinc-deprived have difficulty learning more complex tasks. In infant rats, mild maternal zinc deficiency has been linked to impaired memory.

Human studies done in Sweden have associated low maternal zinc levels in early pregnancy with premature birth, abnormal labor, and bleeding; in mid-pregnancy, with complications at delivery, delayed birth, and congenital malformation of the fetus. That poor maternal zinc levels might adversely affect the outcome of the pregnancy is not surprising—many enzymes, including those concerned with cell multiplication, require zinc for their normal activity.

According to the National Academy of Sciences, Nutritional

TABLE 24

Good Food Sources of Zinc

FOOD	SERVING SIZE	ZINC (mg)
Applesauce	1 cup	0.2 - 0.5
Beef, lean	3 1/2 ounces	4.0 - 5.0
Bran	3/4 cup	1.0 - 1.5
Bread, white	2 slices	0.5 - 1.0
Bread, whole wheat	2 slices	1.0 - 1.5
Cheddar cheese	1 ounce	0.5 - 1.0
Chicken breast	3 ounces	0.5 - 1.0
Clams	3 ounces	1.0 - 1.5
Cranberry - apple drink	8 ounces	0.5 - 1.0
Egg	1 medium	0.2 - 0.5
Gefilte fish	3 1/2 ounces	0.2 - 0.5
Lamb	3 1/2 ounces	4.0 - 5.0
Liver	3 ounces	4.0 - 5.0
Mango	1/2 medium	0.2 - 0.5
Milk, whole or skim	8 ounces	0.5 - 1.0
Oysters, Atlantic	3 1/2 ounces	74.7
Oysters, Pacific	3 1/2 ounces	9.4
Pineapple juice	8 ounces	0.2 - 0.5
Popcorn	2 cups	1.0 - 1.5
Pork, lean	3 1/2 ounces	4.0 - 5.0
Potato, cooked	1 medium	0.2 - 0.5
Puffed wheat	1 ounce	0.5 - 1.0
Rice, brown	1 cup	1.0 - 1.5
Rice, white	1 cup	0.5 - 1.0
Tomato	1 medium	0.2 - 0.5
Tuna	3 ounces	0.5 - 1.0
Wheat germ	1 tablespoon	1.0 - 1.5

TABLE 25

Good Food Sources of Folic Acid

FOOD	SERVING SIZE	FOLIC ACID (mcg)
Apple	1 medium	5 - 20
Beans, green	1 cup	20 - 50
Beef, lean	6 ounces	5 - 20
Bread	1 slice	5 - 20
Brewer's yeast	1 tablespoon	100 - 150
Broccoli	2 stalks	100 - 150
Carrot	1 medium	5 - 20
Cheese, hard	1 ounce	5 - 20
Corn	1 medium ear	5 - 20
Cucumber	1 small	20 - 50
Egg	1 large	20 - 50
Grapefruit	1/2 medium	5 - 20
Kidney	3 ounces	20 - 50
Liver	3 ounces	100 - 150
Milk	8 ounces	5 - 20
Mushrooms	3 large	5 - 20
Orange juice	6 ounces	100 - 150
Pork, lean	6 ounces	5 - 20
Potato	1 medium	5 - 20
Sesame seeds	1 tablespoon	5 - 20
Shellfish	6 ounces	20 - 50
Spinach	4 ounces	100 - 150
Squash	2/3 cup	20 - 50
Strawberries	1 cup	20 - 50
Veal, lean	6 ounces	5 - 20
Yogurt	8 ounces	20 - 50

Research Council, the RDA of zinc is 20 mg. throughout pregnancy. You can get this by eating foods like red meat and liver, along with the others listed in Table 24.

Dietary supplementation in tablet form is not usually needed, except in the case of strict vegetarian (vegans) and women with a very low meat intake. Zinc is found in many of the same foods that contain high levels of iron. Therefore, if you do not eat the right foods, and feel you are doing fine by relying on iron supplements to meet your daily iron needs during pregnancy, you may be unknowingly increasing your risk of zinc deficiency.

Folic Acid and Vitamin C

A combined deficiency of folic acid and vitamin C has been linked to spina bifida, a condition in which the infant's spinal cord does not close completely. Such an infant may be stillborn, or may live for only a few days (although surgery can sometimes correct the condition). It is worthwhile taking 100 mg. of vitamin C daily throughout pregnancy to protect yourself from this.

A deficiency in folic acid alone can also cause spina bifida, as well as a slowdown in DNA production and cell multiplication. During a child's brain growth period, brain DNA content is increasing. RNA is continuously being made throughout life and is crucial to the brain's abilities in both children and adults.

Severe folic acid deficiency, as can be seen in pregnant women on poor diets who have been taking oral contraceptives for a long time prior to becoming pregnant, can cause serious malformations of the brain and other organs. Current medical opinion supports routine folic acid supplementation during pregnancy of 400 mcg. daily, bringing a woman's total intake up to the correct 800 mcg. per day, providing she is eating enough of the foods rich in folic acid.

The Infant's Brain—The Effects of Malnutrition

One must feed the growing brain of the infant as carefully as one did the fetus, or abnormalities will result. The effects of severe deficiencies in calories and protein on infants and young children are better known than those which result from more subtle deprivations of nutrients. There are two broad clinical classifications of severe malnutrition in the very young—marasmus and kwashiorkor. Often they overlap in the same child and occur as a mixed syndrome.

Marasmus, the more common of the two, usually occurs during the first year of life. It is seen in infants who are starved, often as a result of being weaned too early or of not receiving enough food of any kind. It can also crop up in infants as a result of severe and prolonged diarrhea. Marasmus is the condition more threatening to brain development because it occurs at an earlier, more critical age. Kwashiorkor is seen in children aged two or three who have been weaned and then put on diets that are high in starch but low in protein.

Marasmus is essentially the result of severe protein and energy malnutrition. It is often accompanied by infection and diarrhea, which exacerbate the condition. Marasmic children are small and thin, with a measurable reduction in the size of the head. Their brains have fewer cells, and the cells have fewer dendrites and myelin content than normal. Behaviorally, marasmic children are highly irritable—they scream and cry frequently. Children suffering from kwashiorkor are glum and disinterested; they neither play nor laugh, and tend to keep themselves isolated from others.

Even when a child is nutritionally cured of marasmus or kwashiorkor, signs of brain growth retardation often remain. There may be developmental deficits in speech and hearing, eye-hand coordination, interpersonal relations, and problem solving ability.

Although these conditions are rarely seen in modern, Western societies, there are pockets of people all over the world who suffer from, or whose children are suffering from, the ill effects of marasmus and kwashiorkor.

Moderate malnutrition among infants is more common in all societies, and can be caused by illness or an inadequate intake of a specific nutrient, such as zinc or iron, during the first two years of life. Such malnutrition also reduces glial cell multiplication, myelination, dendritic growth, and synapse formation. This leads to impaired memory and problem solving ability as well as increased excitability and decreased curiosity. Many people who have mildly subnormal mental faculties suffered from a subtle nutritional deficiency during their early years.

The Growth of Dendrites

By the age of two, 50% of all brain neurons have their full complement of dendrites, the filaments at the ends of a neuron that link it to other neurons. By age six, 70% are in this position. By a person's early twenties, more than 90% of the dendrites are present, but we continue to acquire new dendrites at a very slow rate for the rest of our lives. More dendrites means mores synapses (the connections between neurons) and so a greater potential for learning.

Protein and calorie malnutrition occurring during the time of peak dendrite manufacture results in fewer synapses being made. The subsequent effects on mental functions—poor memory, slower learning capacity, lowered pain threshold—have all been conclusively demonstrated in animal studies.

Since dendrites are growing throughout our lives, we should constantly be supplying our brains with the proper nutritional input, in order to live up to our full mental potential.

Nutrition for the Infant's Growing Brain

The Role of Fat

The human brain, as we have seen, can use only glucose or ketones as its main energy source. During the first three months of life, the infant uses ketones as a source of brain fuel more extensively than does the adult. It is not completely clear how or why this happens, but it is known that the enzymes involved in the breakdown of brain glucose are poorly developed at this time, whereas the enzymes needed to break down and use ketones for energy are highly active.

Ketone bodies are produced by the liver from fatty acids when a person restricts his or her food intake and turns to using body fat for energy. When an infant is receiving breast milk or infant formula, which are both high in fat, its blood ketone levels are relatively high. When the child begins to be weaned at four to six months of age onto solid food, ketone levels slowly decline until they reach the point seen in normal adults. The higher the level of ketones in the infant's blood during the first three months of life, the greater the rate of manufacture of brain myelin.

The myelin sheath insulates the nerve fiber and facilitates the rapid transmission of nerve impulses. Without enough myelin present, we couldn't even walk—the messages just wouldn't pass quickly enough.

Myelination of the central nervous system begins before birth and is complete by about three weeks of age. Fat accounts for about 75 percent of human myelin, with cholesterol being the major component. The essential fatty acid linoleic acid is also needed for the production of normal myelin and it must be obtained through the diet. Proteins account for the remaining 25 percent. Vitamin B_{12} is also necessary for the production of healthy brain myelin.

If a young infant does not get enough fat into his diet, this may reduce the amount of melyin being made in his brain and subsequently lower his mental performance. Even a reduction in only linoleic acid disturbs myelin production, as does a deficiency of vitamin B_{12}—here the myelin's composition may also be altered. This can result in learning disabilities.

Human milk and infant formula provide adequate fats and also enough fatty acids. This is why these two types of infant foods are the ones recommended for the first year of life. Fortified formulas and, for the most part, human milk, also contain enough vitamin B_{12} for proper myelin manufacture. But vegetarian mothers who are breastfeeding must make sure they get at least 6 mcg. of B_{12} a day. They can do this by eating soy-based products, and by taking a B_{12} supplement if necessary.

Skim milk is not recommended for infant diets, and should never take the place of human milk or formula. And although parents are advised to limit the weight gain in a fat baby, putting the infant on any type of reducing plan should be done only under the strict supervision of a pediatrician.

You can see that an infant's body is geared toward getting a high fat intake during the months right after birth. If this fat intake is limited, normal myelination will not occur, and as a result, the infant's learning abilities will be impaired in later years.

The Role of Zinc

As well as being ideal for energy purposes and myelination, human milk has another advantage. It is the best source of zinc for newborn infants. If the baby is bottle-fed, commercially prepared, zinc-enriched infant formula is the preferred form. When solid foods are introduced at about six months of age, the inclusion of purées of red meat or liver in the diet (as soon as it can be tolerated) is wise because it provides a good dietary source of readily available zinc.

The recommended dietary zinc allowance for infancy is 3 mg. daily from birth to six months, and 5 mg. daily from six months to one year. Severe zinc deficiency in infants is very serious. Without zinc, the brain cannot make any type of new cells and so the result of an extreme deficiency would be serious brain growth retardation.

The Role of Iron

Human milk and fortified formulas provide enough iron for a normal infant for the first four months of life. After that time, an additional source (iron-fortified cereal, puréed meats) should be added to the diet to make sure there is enough iron to meet the requirements of the infant's rapidly expanding tissue mass.

Although human milk contains only .3-.5 mg. of iron per quart (two and a half to three and a half cups of breast milk are produced each day), and this amount technically does not meet the infant's daily requirements, the iron from breast milk is very efficiently absorbed and so is adequate, providing that the iron stores with which the infant is born are up to par. (This is why we cautioned pregnant women against being iron-deficient.) By four months of age these iron stores are depleted and need to be supplemented through the diet. This is also a period of rapid brain development, and so a significant reduction in iron stores can lead to iron deficiency and serious brain dysfunctions.

The first year of life is a period of very high iron requirements. The recommended daily iron intake for infants is 0.5 mg./pound of body weight, not to exceed 15 mg. daily. This requirement should be carefully met from four months of age to three years. Despite the fact that iron is not absorbed efficiently from infant formulas, enough iron has been added to meet the needs of the growing infant for the entire first year of life. Cow's milk alone, without fortification, does not provide enough iron for the child's needs.

Behavioral abnormalities have been reported in children with even a mild iron deficiency. Such children tend to be less attentive, have problems concentrating, and are sometimes hyperactive. Once the iron deficiency is corrected, these symptoms usually disappear.

Hyperactivity

A large number of children can be classified as *brain hyperactive*. They show an inability to concentrate or even to sit still. Various people have suggested that diet may play a role in brain hyperactivity, but the issue is in reality a very complex one.

The controversy over food additives and the possible role they play in the development of hyperactivity in children still rages. In 1973, Dr. Benjamin Feingold, a pediatrician and allergist, reported that children diagnosed as being brain hyperactive dramatically improved when placed on a diet free of all food additives.

Subsequent studies compared the additive-free "Feingold Diet" with an equally restricted diet containing food additives. Neither the parents nor the children knew which diet they were receiving. The results of most of these studies confirmed Dr. Feingold's claim that about half of the children did improve. However, it was not due to the removal of food additives, because the same degree of improvement was seen in both groups. The results of another study further confused the issue by showing that there was slightly more improvement in a group of under-three-year-olds who were placed on an additive-free diet. (Hyperactivity, by the way, is rarely found in children that young.)

These results, then, do not indicate that all additives should be removed from the diets of hyperactive children. What they do show is that a change in dietary pattern, with or without the removal of additives, may be of some benefit. There may also be a small number of hyperactive children under the age of three who could improve on an additive-free diet.

Furthermore, some food additives may indeed be capable of producing hyperactivity in children who are sensitive to them. Red dye number 3, which is commonly added to foods, has been shown to increase hyperactivity for a short period of time in already hyperactive children, when administered in large amounts.

Parents of brain hyperactive children may notice that the ingestion of foods with a very high sugar content tend to make the child worse. No one has yet proven this or explained why it is so. In addition, associations made between heightened brain activity and high-carbohydrate diets are difficult to interpret, as carbohydrates affect not only blood sugar levels but the levels of neurotransmitters like serotonin as well.

Environment and Nutrition

Prenatal nutrition, or the lack of it, can have lasting and serious effects on the growing brain. Postnatally, behavior can also be affected by malnutrition, but the effects may not be permanent, unless the environment is also deprived.

Children's brains should be stimulated with enough sights, sounds, smells, toys, and conversation to develop normally. The combination of poor malnutrition and poor environmental stimulation has a very damaging effect on the brain of a young child. Children who were exposed to both dietary and environmental deprivation showed lower IQ scores and poorer school performances. However, it was found that environmental enrichment can reverse many of the behavioral abnormalities caused by the combination of early malnutrition and environmental deprivation.

In Conclusion

The relationship between nutrition and the functioning of the brain from gestation through infancy is just beginning to be understood. Nevertheless, we know that the influence of the diet is substantial. Proper human nutrition must begin in the womb and continue throughout life. Adequate amounts of the vital nutrients that both brain and body need must be consumed by the mother during pregnancy, and must be fed to the infant after birth, especially during the first three years of his or her life. It will make all the difference, in the long run, to the child's mental capabilities.

How To Cope

During pregnancy:
- Protein: 74 gm. daily from food
- Iron: 30-60 mg. supplement (ferrous sulfate) daily, taken with meals
- Zinc: 20 mg. daily from food
- Folic acid: 400 mcg. supplement daily
- Vitamin C: 80mg. daily from food.

Infant, birth to 3 years:
- Fat
- Linoleic acid
- Vitamin B_{12} birth to 6 months 0.5 mcg.; 6 months to 1 year 1.5 mcg.; 1-3 years 2 mcg.
- Zinc: birth to 6 months 3 mg. supplement daily; 6 months to 1 year 5 mg.
- Iron: 4 months to 3 years 0.5 mg. per pound of body weight daily (maximum 15 mg.)

CHAPTER 11

Nutrition for the Aging Brain

Do the functions and capacities of our brains actually slow down and become less efficient as we age? Is senility a necessary evil of growing older? Or can the right diet, with the proper environmental stimulation, keep us mentally sharp throughout our lives? The answer to the last question, in most cases, is emphatically yes.

Carl and Marie were a happy couple in their mid-70s, enjoying the best of health. They celebrated their 50th wedding anniversary with much to be thankful for, and with the expectation of many more years together. Now that Carl had retired from his civil service job, they were able to do all the things together they hadn't had time for in the past. They filled the days with each other's company—going to movies and museums, and taking vacations.

Nine months after their anniversary, Marie died suddenly from a massive heart attack. Carl was devastated. His son, Alex, who lived in a nearby state, tried to convince his father to leave his painful roots behind and come to live with Alex and his family. But Carl felt it would be an unwise move and feared that he would soon become a burden to his son.

Carl lost interest in almost everything. He stopped going out and doing the things he used to do with Marie—the memories were simply too painful for him. One memory in particular haunted him. In Marie's house, mealtimes were always festive occasions, as they both enjoyed eating good food. Marie loved showing off her culinary skills, and Carl enjoyed making her feel appreciated by cleaning his plate.

Now that Marie was dead, Carl didn't see any reason to care about what he ate—anything simple and small would do. He had never prepared the meals before and had no desire to learn how to do so now. Sometimes he skipped eating altogether.

Carl also eventually stopped shaving, didn't bathe very often, and in general let himself and his house go to ruin. His neighbors finally wrote Alex, who came to see his father. For the three days that Alex stayed, Carl put up a good show, eating regularly, bathing, etc. He was afraid of either becoming a burden to his son or of being sent to a "home." However, when Alex left, Carl felt lonelier than ever and started to drink to ease his painful memories of happier days with Marie.

Over the next two years, Carl drank more and more and ate less and less. Every time Alex visited he saw that his father was slowly deteriorating, but Carl refused to discuss it. Alex found unpaid bills that Carl had forgotten about, piles of unwashed clothing, and a broken oven. He also noticed that his father seemed to be getting much thinner.

On the second anniversary of his mother's death, Alex went to see his father in order to try to force him to come live with him. He found Carl in an alarming state. His father was confused and disoriented, as well as highly irritable, often blowing up at the least little thing. He also seemed to have difficulty walking, and his ankles were swollen. Carl was a completely different person from the mild-mannered, loving father Alex remembered. Alex called his wife, Nora. "My father, I'm afraid, is completely senile now," he sadly told her. "I'm taking him to the hospital here in the morning."

Carl's physicians quickly found the root of the trouble and all his strange symptoms. It was not senility. Instead, Carl was suffering from a severe deficiency in vitamin B_1. After just a few days of B_1 therapy, Carl began to improve dramatically. He was no longer confused and hostile, and no longer had problems walking.

Six months later he joined his local chapter of Alcoholics Anonymous where he is now meeting new people, learning to enjoy life again, and developing better eating habits. He is even contemplating moving in with his son and daughter-in-law in the future, but there is no rush now. No longer does Carl's future look so irreversibly bleak, nor is he any longer considered "senile."

Carl had actually been suffering from vitamin B_1 deficiency for quite some time, due to his poor diet, exacerbated by his use of alcohol, which increased his body's need for the vitamin.

Carl's story, unfortunately, is not uncommon. What is often mistaken for senility—symptoms of forgetfulness, irritability, and a loss of identity—and what is popularly considered to be the necessary result of growing old, is often not a serious or irreversible condition at all. It can be caused by many things, and may indeed not be the result of a real physical ailment such as hardening of the arteries of the brain. In fact, more often than not, so-called senility is often caused by a poor diet, which can easily be corrected. The human brain never stops needing its full supply of the proper nutrients daily.

The Aging Brain: What Happens?

Does the brain deteriorate? To some degree, it does. But does this have to affect our behavior and thought? If the proper diet is followed and no abnormal disease state is present, the answer is no.

There is no reason why a person's brain cannot be as alert and healthy during older age as it was during youth. The rate at which oxygen and blood flow through the brains of healthy elderly people is no different from the rate at which it flows in normal young people. Thus, it is a myth that hardening of the arteries is a natural condition of older age. A healthy lifestyle, which includes exercise and the right diet, can prevent arteriosclerosis. Genetic tendencies do play a part in our relative health, but even these can be eased or even overcome.

Furthermore, tests of brain activity suggest that the healthy aged brain works just as hard and efficiently as the healthy young brain. In fact, due to experience and learning, some studies have shown that older people are actually more intelligent than younger people.

Still, destructive changes do occur in the brain and body as one ages, though they need not show in the behavior. In th normal aging process, the brain shrinks about 10-15 percent due to the death of brain cells and destruction of dendrites. But since we have so many brain cells and dendrites to begin with, the brain appears to be able to compensate for this loss.

During the first 50-60 years of life, the majority of cells that die are located in the cortex. Actually, from the age of 20 onward, 50,000 nerve cells each day are lost, mainly from this area. At the same time, some parts of the brain continue to grow as long as we live. Dendrites, for instance, are lost continuously, but also grow constantly.

Normal elderly people appear to have a built-in protective mechanism in their brains that compensates for the loss of cells so that this loss is rarely noticed. However, one cannot deny that many elderly people do seem to think and move more slowly. It would seem, then, that at a certain point, depending on the state of health, genetic tendency, and the actual age, the brain cells that are regressing and dying begin to outnumber the cells that are surviving and growing. The right diet is one way to help delay this process.

By the age of 65, 10% of all noninstitutionalized Americans, and 20% of those over the age of 75, do show substantial intellectual impairment—demonstrating that their brains are no longer able to compensate for the cellular losses. Some of these people have neglected their health—by eating the wrong foods, getting little or no exercise, abusing alcohol or drugs, exerting too much stress on their bodies—and are possibly paying for it in their old age.

The loss of brain cells in everyone is believed to be responsible for the natural aging of the body. Specifically, losses from the hypothalamus unbalance the metabolic conditions. The hypothalamus controls the hormonal system, which regulates the rate at which the body works and affects almost all bodily functions. It is so important to our well-being that if it stopped working completely, the entire body would malfunction. Because of its critical role, many have called the hypothalamus our "biological clock." Anything that speeds up its deterioration will speed up the aging process. For example, studies have shown that a high-protein diet accelerates the biological clock. This is one of the reasons nutritionists recommend that we limit our daily protein intake to only 13% of all calories consumed.

During aging, the brain is also less able to make protein, and hence, enzymes. This results in an impaired ability to break down and use glucose as well as other vital nutrients. This means that the brain is creating less energy, and thus is working less efficiently and more slowly. But again, providing that the person is eating well and living a healthy life, this effect can be delayed, sometimes indefinitely. Also, this process is not uniform throughout the brain. In different brain regions, according to the person, preferential decreases may occur while other areas remain unaffected.

In each case, an excess or deficit of a specific neurotransmitter, as we have mentioned, can be directly reflected in a behavioral change. For instance, the reduced level of serotonin often found in the elderly brain is undoubtedly responsible for the depression so commonly seen. Normal brain functions depend on a delicate balance of neurotransmitters and any disturbance in this equilibrium can have notable repercussions. For example, the reduced production of dopamine by the neurons in one region means that there is now an excess level of acetylcholine present. This situation causes problems with movement. But once again, as food affects neurotransmitter levels, the right diet, targeted for the specific problems of an individual's brain, can offset many unpleasant symptoms of growing old. Unfortunately, older people are often the most negligent when it comes to following a well-balanced, consistently consumed meal plan.

Eating Problems of the Elderly

Today, approximately 25 million people, or 11% of the U.S. population, are over the age of 65. By the year 2025, there will be 42 million older Americans, or 16 percent of the population. The simple reason for this is that people are living longer, while the birth rate is decreasing. Therefore, it makes sense that we should pay more and more attention to this too frequently forgotten sector of our nation.

The majority of older people complain of such mentally related problems as:

- forgetfulness
- fatigue
- poor muscle coordination
- irritability
- depression
- lethargy

All these symptoms can be lessened, and in some cases erased, by the proper diet. Of course, no issue is ever as simple as it sounds. Many causes for these problems do not come from, nor can they be corrected by, the diet, but we deal with these later in this chapter. For the most part, people over the age of 65 simply stop eating balanced meals and therefore suffer because of it.

To begin with, they often have dental problems, which makes chewing more difficult. This can be remedied by preparing food in a "soft" way, and by avoiding foods that are hard to chew or swallow.

Second, since eyesight often becomes poorer as we age, the pleasure that people receive from seeing a "colorful" plate of food is gone and everything now just looks like a muddy shade of gray—and unappetizing. This can be remedied by wearing reading glasses while eating, and by taking meals in a well-lit room.

People living alone, like Carl, often skip meals, especially if they are widowed and therefore unaccustomed to eating alone. They feel there is no reason to cook anymore. "Why should I go to all that trouble just for myself?" they protest. The first solution to this problem is to change our attitudes toward being alone—it can be a rewarding time, a time to start over and make new friends. One can also encourage the older person to *make* friends and have meals with them, or to eat at senior citizen centers.

Another problem is that many older people claim that they do not enjoy eating anymore because all food tastes the same, or because everything tastes so bland. This is not surprising; older age often brings with it a reduction in the sense of taste, better known as a loss of taste acuity. Often, this problem is simply due to a deficiency in zinc, and the administration of 15 mg. per day of a zinc supplement can bring the taste buds back to life.

Still, the largest single problem that older people encounter when it comes to eating is their reduced ability to digest and absorb food.

Digestive Disorders

With age, the ability to absorb and use certain nutrients decreases. The absorptive cells of the intestines, for example, lose some of their efficiency in taking nutrients from digested food. The lining of the small intestine becomes thinner, with fewer absorptive cells, along with fewer blood vessels to carry nutrients to other parts of the body.

This decreased ability to use vital nutrients is also partly due to the fact that older people produce less gastric acid and fewer digestive enzymes in their stomachs. This decreased acid production interferes with iron and vitamin B_{12} absorption, both of which are needed to prevent anemia.

How many of these digestive substances are lost with age varies considerably from person to person. Some people maintain the same rate of acid secretion they had in their youth, while others produce almost no acid. Why this type of difference exists is still not known.

Another physical age change is a reduction in the secretion of digestive juices by the gall bladder, the pancreas, and the small intestine. This loss inhibits a person's ability to digest fat and can cause gas to build up. Heartburn is another common complaint. Unfortunately, most older people take these two symptoms to mean that they have hyperacidic stomachs.

The diet can certainly be of some help in avoiding this syndrome. Substances such as fat, chocolate, alcohol, peppermint, cigarettes, and various drugs can aggravate gaseous build-up and heartburn. People who mistakenly believe that these symptoms come from too much acid in the stomach often take antacids in excess. This can prove dangerous to the brain, as many of these products contain aluminum hydroxide, and numerous studies have shown that aluminum can encourage senility. Antacids also make digestive problems worse; these tablets neutralize what little acid is still present and completely disrupt the digestion of food. Other types of antacids, such as those based on calcium carbonate, increase the likelihood of constipation—another common complaint of the elderly.

Half of the United States population can expect to develop constipation and diverticulosis in old age. Both disorders can be modified or helped by diet. Diverticulosis is a condition in which diverticuli, or pouches, form in the wall of the large intestine, causing gas pockets to develop. They are mainly caused by eating a diet low in fiber, which forces the muscles to strain in order to empty the contents of the intestine. Eating plenty of bulky fiber—found in bran (if taken with water), vegetables, whole grain foods such as brown rice, whole grain bread, and similar products, prevents this problem.

However, elderly people often instead use and abuse laxatives to clear up the constipation problem. This leads to the loss of essential vitamins and minerals through the stool. Some of the nutrients lost in this way, such as potassium and calcium, are essential to normal brain function.

The Right Diet

Elderly people need a balanced, healthy daily diet, just like at any other stage of life—and maybe even more so, to help them recover from injuries or illnesses.

As a person gets older, the amount of muscle tissue present decreases and the rate at which the body conducts its overall processes slows down. So, just as less sleep is needed, fewer calories (or energy) are required from the diet.

This decreases in caloric consumption, however, must be adjusted according to how active the person is.

A moderately active person walks sometimes rather than always using the car to get around, stands frequently, and engages in some household chores and light exercise. These people need to decrease their caloric intake by 5 percent for each decade between the ages of 40 to 60; by 10 percent for the decade between 60 and 70; and by another 10 percent for the years over 70.

A lightly active person rarely walks, sits down as much as possible, and gets little or no exercise. Caloric intake in this case should be decreased by 5 percent for the decade between 40 to 50 years of age; by 10 percent from 50 to 60; by 10 percent from 60 to 70; and by 10 percent over the age of 70.

A heavily active person exercises regularly. In this case, the person's own body weight must be his or her guide. If you are holding steady at your lifelong weight, you don't need to decrease your calories. If you are gaining weight, cut down on caloric intake in the same proportions that moderately active person would.

The diet must be adjusted in this way to compensate for the metabolic changes occurring within the body. However, a failure to reduce the amount you eat can lead to obesity, which increases the risk of developing arteriosclerosis, a condition that can be devastating to brain health.

Age-Related Diseases—Can They Be Eased or Corrected by the Diet?

Not all the ailments mentioned in this section can be cured simply by altering the diet; some can be helped, some may only be slightly affected. In any case, if you exhibit symptoms of a serious ailment, you should always see a physician before trying a home or dietary cure alone. You may need medication or treatment. however, one thing is true in the case of all these ailments—the right diet can never *hurt* in the treatment of any disease. On the other hand, some of the diseases mentioned here are caused purely by an improper diet, and the symptoms should disappear with the correct type of nutrient supplementation.

All of the following diseases to some extent affect brain function. Even digestive ailments, such as the ones mentioned earlier, prevent the body from properly absorbing nutrients. The brain, as we have seen over and over again, cannot function properly without its full complement of nutrients consumed on a daily basis.

Arteriosclerosis

Heart disease. Hardening of the arteries. We all know about it. Many of us even *expect* it to come with advancing age. Well, this needn't be the case, and even if it does happen, heart disease can be controlled and its advancement slowed, instead of being allowed to run its inevitable course toward death.

147

Arteriosclerosis, or hardening of the arteries, caused by deposits of cholesterol lining the blood vessels does not, unfortunately, affect only the heart, as some people think. Susan was a woman in her late sixties who was not surprised to learn that she had arteriosclerosis. Her parents and both brothers had already died from it. But since she didn't have much pain, she tried to ignore it. Her diet remained the same, she didn't exercise, and she rarely took the medication her doctor had prescribed.

Susan bragged that her heart disease was obviously not as bad as everybody thought, since she felt fine. But her friends started to notice other problems. Susan was becoming extremely forgetful, disoriented, and frequently hostile. Her arteries were clogged up not only around her heart, but in her head as well. She didn't know that arteriosclerosis can sometimes cause mental impairment due to the decreased supply of oxygen going to the brain.

This whole syndrome could have been combatted had Susan taken her medication and made certain modifications in her lifestyle. People with arteriosclerosis (and even those without it who want to prevent its onset) should first of all reduce their intake of animal fat. The advance of heart disease can be slowed down by eating a diet that contains a one to one (1:1) ratio of animal fat to vegetable fat. In addition, these people should eat *pectin* (found in apples, oranges, and grapefruit), and a lot of fish (foods that have been shown to lower blood cholesterol levels). Regular exercise is another essential step, even if you just walk every day. It has been shown that exercise, if done three times a week or more, increases the amount of oxygen going to the brain by as much as 30 percent, in addition to strengthening the heart and lungs.

However, use your own judgment when it comes to deciding how much exercise is too much. Nine hours of tennis for a person with arteriosclerosis is not helpful; it is harmful. The best way to map out a personally suited exercise program is to see your physician and let him do it, based on what he knows about the overall state of your body.

Another dietary tip doesn't involve a food, but rather a common household drug. Taking aspirin every other day appears to be beneficial. The aspirin prevents platelets from sticking together. Platelets are the tiny blood cells that are involved in blood clotting and that are a significant component part of the plaque that builds up in the arteries.

Anemia

Anemia simply means that your red blood cell count is low. This can result in fatigue, lethargy, shortness of breath when the body is exerted, and a rapid heartbeat. Headaches, the loss of concentration, depression, and irritability are all early warning signals.

Anemia is a common problem among the elderly because of their inadequate intake of iron, folic acid, and vitamin B_{12}, coupled with their reduced ability to absorb iron. Therefore, make sure that you eat foods that are rich in these nutrients on a daily basis. One portion of liver a week would be ideal. Iron is also abundant in red meat, enriched bread, raisins, and beans, although the iron obtained from meat is absorbed in greater quantity than the iron absorbed from plant sources—10 percent as opposed to 5 percent, respectively. Hence, if little meat is eaten, it may be a good idea to take a 10 mg. supplement of iron daily.* Folic acid can be obtained from green leafy vegetables, beans, peas, and, once again, liver.

One vitamin that's often negatively associated with aging is vitamin B_{12}. It is common practice to give the elderly a "booster injection" of this vitamin. B_{12} is a special case, in that its absorption by the body depends on something called the *intrinsic factor*—a chemical found in the secretions of the stomach—which takes the vitamin B_{12} across the wall of the small intestine and into the bloodstream.

---

*A few people may be at risk for an iron overload. If you have anemia for some reason other than iron deficiency, cirrhosis, Parkinson's disease, or have been taking iron supplements for several years, check with your doctor before taking any more iron supplements. This is especially true for men, who do not lose iron over their lifetimes through menstrual bleeding, and are therefore more likely to retain high body levels of iron. Too much iron in the diet can cause iron deposits in the liver, pancreas, heart, and skin, and can be dangerous to overall physical health. Symptoms of an overload usually show up after the age of 40, and one of the first signs is the development of a bronze cast to the skin. Left untreated, iron overload can cause the pancreas to malfunction (resulting in diabetes), as well as the liver (upsetting the whole metabolism of the body), and can eventually lead to death.

With advancing age, most people produce a little less of this substance, and a few older people produce too little. Without the intrinsic factor, no dietary vitamin B_{12} can be absorbed and used by the body. So individuals who severely lack the intrinsic factor may require B_{12} injections to prevent both anemia and the degeneration of brain myelin that B_{12} deficiency causes. But this condition is rare, and almost everyone who eats red meat twice a week has approximately a three to five year store of B_{12} in his or her liver. Thus, B_{12} injections do not provide quick energy, and while they are not harmful (except for the expense), they help very few people. If you do not eat much meat in your diet or any supplemented vegetable products (such as tofu), you should take a daily 6 mcg. supplement of vitamin B_{12}.

Senile dementia

The disease known as senile dementia affects 15% of the United States population over the age of 64, and is the fourth leading cause of death in this country. The symptoms are well known: memory impairment, slowness of movement and thought, confusion, amnesia, feelings of disorientation, extreme lethargy, paranoia, inflexibility, and a resistance to any sort of change. In fact, the avoidance or fear of change is an early warning sign that a person may have the ailment. People with this disease lose brain cells at a rate much faster than normal.

There are many different types of senile dementia, and each demands a different type of therapeutic attention. Of all the people who suffer from the symptoms mentioned, about 50% are victims of *Alzheimer's disease*. Twenty to 30% may be suffering from a combination of Alzheimer's disease and another type of senility known as *multi-infarct dementia*, or from multi-infarct dementia alone.

In multi-infarct dementia, a series of imperceptible and minor strokes destroy significant amounts of brain tissue. Hypertensive people are the most susceptible to this condition. Of course, nutrition has a big part to play in the control of hypertension, or high blood pressure. To guard against it, cut down on salt intake and boost potassium intake. In practical terms, this means that no salt should be added to meals, but up to one teaspoon per day can be used during cooking. Pickled food, such sauerkraut, and extremely salty foods, like luncheon meats, chips, and processed cheese should also be avoided. Foods that should be accented in the diet are those which are rich, in potassium, such as citrus fruit, spinach, raisins, almonds, and avocados.

At one time many doctors believed that hardening of the arteries was the major cause of senile dementia. In fact, arteriosclerosis in the brain is only one of the many vascular disorders that can result in dementia. Any blockage that deprives the brain of blood and oxygen can cause small strokes and eventually dementia.

The remaining 20 to 30% of senile patients may be suffering from any one of a number of reversible physical conditions that result in serious, but often temporary, changes in memory or intellect. They could include:

- fevers
- infections
- metabolic disorders, like hypo- or hyperthyroidism
- toxic reactions to drugs, such as the type that cause abnormal drops in blood glucose levels
- deficiency of vitamin B_1, often caused by the excess consumption of alcohol
- deficiency of vitamin B_{12}, which leads to myelin degeneration
- deficiency of folic acid and niacin
- alcohol and drug abuse

All these conditions can upset the normal functioning of a person's sensitive brain cells. If left untreated, such ailments can cause permanent brain damage and even death.

The other type of dementia we mentioned is Alzheimer's disease. Early studies showed that if one member of your family has this disease you possess a four-times greater risk of contracting it yourself when you get older. Some researchers feel that it is caused by a slow-acting virus, while others believe that the immune systems of some older people lose their ability to recognize elements of their own bodies, including the nerve cells, and begin to attack them and break them down.

Unfortunately, there is not much you can do about your genetic makeup or about a virus. However, other factors have been cited that could contribute to the onset of Alzheimer's disease, and they can be controlled. Aluminum has been implicated in aggravating this disease, as well as other forms of senile dementia. You should therefore, avoid, throughout your life, cooking or eating with aluminum pots and utensils and should also not abuse aluminum-containing antacids. Alzheimer's disease, by the way, is one of the earliest occurring forms of senility. It can strike down people as young as 50.

Another characteristic of senility is the brain's reduced ability to produce acetylcholine, by as much as 70 to 80 percent. Acetycholine is the neurotransmitter responsible for memory. You can increase the levels of acetylcholine in your brain by taking a daily supplement of one to two grams of choline in the form of lecithin (30 grams of lecithin are needed). This type of therapy is most effective in treating people with Alzheimer's disease if they have had the disease for less than three years.

Depression

The elderly are reported to be at a two- to three-fold greater risk for the development of severe depression. Emotional problems such as depression are unfortunately often confused with irreversible brain diseases, such as senile dementia.

Depression, loss of self-esteem, loneliness, anxiety, and boredom are more common in elderly people especially after they retire, or when they experience the deaths of relatives and friends. Their own health problems may upset them emotionally as well.

Some of this depression is caused by a change in the brain's chemistry. The loss of serotonin-containing neurons, the increasing degradation of this neurotransmitter that affects the emotions, as well as the inefficient use by the brain of the serotonin that is present seem to be responsible for depression.

Jeanine was always happy and fun-loving. She had a career as an interior decorator, which she loved, a husband who adored her, and loads of friends. But as she reached her late sixties, depression began to overtake her more and more. At first, she convinced herself that it was understandable. Her husband had died three years earlier, and now her two best friends were also gone. Because of a slight heart condition and painful arthritis, she had decided to sell her business and retire.

Jeanine was not one to allow the depression to rule her life and make her an invalid, however. She traveled to places she had always wanted to see, and made new friends. Yet the depression persisted and deepened. She finally sought the help of a physician.

The doctor promptly explained to Jeanine that her depression might be caused by a minor and common chemical imbalance in the brain. He called it a lack of serotonin, and instructed her to take two to three grams of tryptophan daily, which she easily found in her nearby vitamin store. Within a few weeks, she was already feeling more like her old self.

Tryptophan, the substance that makes serotonin in the brain, has been shown to alleviate many depressive symptoms. Meanwhile, it is important for families and physicians to recognize this relatively "normal" depression seen in the elderly and to distinguish its symptoms from those of senile dementia.

Parkinson's Disease

Approximately 500,000 people in this country over the age of 50 are suspected of having Parkinson's disease. Its symptoms include trembling of the limbs, muscular stiffness, and slow body movements. Sufferers may also stand with a stooped posture, walk with short, shuffling steps, and speak softly in a rapid, even tone at all times.

The trembling most commonly associated with the disease usually affects the hands and feet. It shows up when the limb is resting, and disappears when the limb is moving. For example, the trembling in the hand will stop when the person reaches out to pick up an object, but will return when the hand is returned to a resting position.

The muscular stiffness is called "plastic rigidity" because the muscles seem unable to relax. They also exhibit resistance to passive manipulation, such as when a doctor raises an arm. The slow body movements are caused by the person's hesitancy to initiate new movements, and also result in rapid fatiguing. This causes a reduction in many movements that we are normally unaware of, such as the blinking of our eyes, the slight swinging of our arms when we walk, and our execution of subtle facial expressions.

What causes the disease? Parkinson's disease is due to a problem with a group of nerve cells in the brain that form a nucleus called the *substantia nigra*. Substantia nigra means "black substance," and is so named because the nerve cells are packed with dark-colored pigment granules. These granules appear to have something to do with the fact that these neurons produce and store the neurotransmitter dopamine, which carries messages of movement.

The nerve cells of the substantia nigra send long, thin fibers upward to connect with nerve cells in an area of the gray matter known as the *corpus striatum*. The dopamine made in the cells of the substantia nigra travels up these fibers to the corpus striatum and on arrival transmits nerve impulses that control movement to the neurons in that area.

When the cells in the substantia nigra are impaired they cannot make dopamine and so a deficiency results in the corpus striatum. When this deficiency becomes severe enough, symptoms of Parkinson's disease begin to appear.

While many scientists say that Parkinsonism is due to the depletion of brain dopamine, the real cause of the disease is still unknown. Some speculate that it is due to a virus, while others theorize that a premature aging process attacks the cells of the substantia nigra. However, despite popular belief, the disease does not appear to be genetically linked.

Parkinson's disease usually starts at about 60 years of age, and its onset is marked by a slight feeling of weakness in the limbs and trembling in an arm or hand. The symptoms increase gradually over a long period of time.

How is the disease treated? There is no cure for Parkinson's disease at this point. The symptoms are treated mainly through the use of drugs. The best way to improve the function of the "sick" dopamine-producing nerve cells is to take L-DOPA (levodopa), which is converted in the brain to dopamine. The drugs used in the treatment of the disease act either by replenishing brain dopamine or by modifying brain function in order to compensate for dopamine deficiency. The presence of acetylcholine is another contributing factor to the disease. This neurotransmitter, which is responsible for short-term memory, is also found in large amounts in the corpus striatum but, unlike dopamine, its supply is not limited by the disease. As a matter of fact, there seems to be a reciprocal "see-saw" relationship between these two chemical messengers and their nerve cells. Dopamine normally restrains the acetylcholine-containing cells. In Parkinson's disease these nerve cells are released from their restraints. Their consequently improperly regulated activity appears to contribute to the symptoms of the disease. Therefore, drugs that inhibit the action of acetylcholine ease the symptoms of the disease.

Nutrition and Parkinson's disease

This disease is not caused by a nutritional deficiency, and no type of food can be used to treat or cure it. Consequently, any claims made by unqualified sources about nutritional cures should be ignored. However, food can tamper with the effectiveness of the medications, and levodopa should always be taken after a meal containing solid food, or else it can cause nausea.

Protein: A high-protein meal, like a steak dinner, can reduce the absorption of levodopa. This doesn't mean that if you are on this medication you have to restrict your intake of protein. It means that your doctor should adjust your dosage to conform to your normal diet. A low-protein diet (which is the most beneficial type, anyway, for older people) indicates the need for a lower dosage, and vice versa. Obviously your diet must be kept consistent. Eat meals at regular times, and try to avoid dietary excesses or "surprises."

Tyrosine: Some faddists claim that taking in large amounts of tyrosine, an amino acid found mainly in the proteins we eat, will help the disease, since the brain makes levodopa from tyrosine. Actually, this doesn't work, for two reasons. First of all, patients with Parkinson's disease don't seem to be able to convert tyrosine into levodopa very efficiently. Second, most of the tyrosine we get from our diets is used to build new protein. Only a very small amount is taken up from the blood by the neurons in the substantia nigra and the other neurons in the body that make dopamine. Thus, tyrosine has little effect in treating the disease.

155

Vitamin B$_6$: Don't believe the claims that this vitamin helps cure the symptoms of the disease—it actually makes them worse.

Only 1 percent of any dose of L-DOPA reaches the brain. Vitamin B$_6$ is essential for the optimal function of the enzymes (located in the nerve tissues throughout the body) that control the conversion of L-DOPA to dopamine. If a person with Parkinson's disease takes vitamin B$_6$ supplements, this action of the enzymes will convert L-DOPA to dopamine at a much faster rate. So, what's wrong with that? Well, it converts it so quickly that it changes it all to dopamine before the L-DOPA has the chance even to reach the brain! Dopamine, unfortunately, cannot enter the brain and so people on levodopa find their symptoms exacerbated when they take vitamin supplements containing vitamin B$_6$. You must avoid tablets that contain more than the minimum daily requirement of B$_6$ (0.51 mg. per day). One food—wheat germ—naturally contains enough B$_6$ to partly reverse the effects of levodopa, so it should be eliminated from the diet, as well.

Tryptophan: Many people use tryptophan supplements to relieve common depression and help them sleep. It is a naturally occurring amino acid and it makes serotonin in the same way that tyrosine makes levodopa in the brain. Serotonin is also present in the substantia nigra along with dopamine. The two appear to be antagonistic to each other. Some reports state that large doses of tryptophan exacerbate the symptoms of Parkinson's disease, so this is another form of supplement that should be avoided.

Choline: Choline in the form of lecithin is taken by some people to improve memory. However, because of the negative reciprocal relationship mentioned earlier between dopamine and acetylcholine (which is made from choline), it is a good idea for people with Parkinson's disease to stay away from choline supplements. Increasing the formation of acetylcholine exacerbates the symptoms of the disease.

Phenylalanine: Some sufferers of Parkinson's disease have tried taking an amino acid found in health food stores called phenylalanine. Dr. George Cotzias of Buenos Aires reported that D-phenylalanine was somewhat effective in controlling the tremors in several patients. There are two problems here, however. First, we know little about any toxic effects on the body that might result from taking D-phenylalanine for any period of time. Second, health food stores do not carry D-phenylalanine, they carry L-phenylalanine. The L-form has no beneficial effects on the symptoms of Parkinson's disease.

Salt: Sodium chloride or table salt may be helpful in combating one of the side effects seen in some people who take levodopa—low blood pressure, which results in fatigue and/or dizziness. Usually one to two grams per day should do the trick. While this is more than you would get from just adding salt to your food, the average American (unless he is on a salt-free diet) takes in much more than this through his normal meals. However, there is a caution here. Excess salt intake can be dangerous to overrall physical health. It can cause or increase high blood pressure, can exacerbate chronic congestive heart failure, and may result in kidney problems. Therefore, let your doctor decide whether you need to increase your intake of salt.

Sleep Disorders

Many older people complain that they are not getting enough sleep because they are sleeping only six hours. But this is normal for this age group. Others, however, really do have problems in sleeping. Older people tend to wake up more frequently during the night, spend less time in REM or deep sleep, and so do not feel well rested in the morning.

The simple and highly effective remedy is to take two or three grams of tryptophan before bedtime. This raises brain serotonin levels, the neurotransmitter that controls, among other things, the level of sleepiness or wakefulness. It is completely safe (except for people with Parkinson's disease, as mentioned), is free from side effects, and is nonaddictive, which is certainly more than can be said for chemical sleep preparations such as tranquilizers, sleeping pills, and hypnotics. However check with your doctor before taking tryptophan on a regular basis.

Memory Problems

Of the 25 million older people in this country, only 3 to 4 million suffer from intellectual problems. Of these, only a small fraction are so severely affected that they can no longer take care of themselves.

Although forgetfulness most commonly afflicts the elderly, people can experience it at any age. Therefore, older people should not become too upset if they cannot remember relatively unimportant information. There is little need for worry if the name, date, or place of an experience is forgotten—as long as the experience itself is recalled, providing that the experience was an important one. Few people will remember three years later that on a certain day they said hello to the mailman while he was crossing the road. It is only when an important experience is totally forgotten, or when forgetfulness causes the person to become unable to deal with family, friends, or daily responsibilities that medical care should be sought.

The memory problems may be caused by difficulties in acquiring new information, storing it away with all the learned items acquired over a lifetime, and then having to retrieve the new information quickly. Visual or hearing problems can make the situation worse. A lack of concentration or even motivation can also prevent the proper acquisition of new information.

For example, when you enter a library, your brain is actually receiving dozens of signals at one time, and so you must selectively choose the data you need in order to find the book you want. Imagine an elderly person with short-term memory problems who finds himself in the same situation. He enters the library looking for two books. Suddenly, there is a loud noise, a lot of screaming and yelling in the vicinity, and the man sees that a fight is taking place between youths. The guards come, the fight is broken up, but now the man can remember only one of the two titles he came to the library to obtain.

Reaction speed may also decrease with age. Thus, even if information is properly acquired and stored, a person may be slower in sifting through his or her data banks in order to recover that information from memory. The man in the library may well remember the other book title on the way home, but not at the moment he needed the information to come quickly back to him.

Many other people also complain that their minds are

cluttered with unwanted thoughts that frequently intrude on their line of conversation or the subject they are trying to think about. However, none of these age-related changes becomes a real problem until extreme old age, and sometimes not even then. Older people can compensate for the small degree of memory loss they may be experiencing by:

- keeping notes or lists
- making sure they have adequate uninterrupted time in which to learn new things
- concentrating on one thing at a time
- being surrounded by good lighting and good acoustics
- not becoming upset it they cannot remember things as quickly as they could when they were younger—because they probably remember them just as well, just at a slightly slower rate

A loss of the ability to produce acetylcholine, especially in the hippocampus section of the brain, which regulates memory, may be a key factor in the memory loss experienced by the elderly. Drugs that preserve the limited supplies of acetylcholine have had a positive effect on people suffering from age-related memory loss, as well as from Alzheimer's disease. *Physostigmine* is one drug that is now being used successfully in several medical centers. However, it cannot be used over long periods of time, since it has been shown to cause irreversible damage to the nerve cells. Dietary supplements of choline, one of the main elements necessary for the manufacture of acetylcholine, may be beneficial. Thirty grams a day of lecithin (in the form of phosphatidylcholine) needs to be taken. It is probably best, because of the large amount, to obtain it in a powdered form and add it to food and drinks, instead of taking all those tablets. However, the results of choline therapy at this time have not been that encouraging, except for patients with Alzheimer's disease.

Vitamin E Treatments: Cells in the aging brain collect a substance called *lipofuscin* (or age pigment), which is made when oxygen combines with polyunsaturated fats in the neurons. The mass of pigment displaces other integral parts of the cell that are necessary for normal function, and it can lead to the death of some of the dendrites.

Some researchers feel that it is lipofuscin that hinders

normal neuronal function, based on studies that linked its accumulation to the impairment of short-term memory in animals.

Vitamin E is an antioxidant, that is, it can prevent oxygen from altering the structure of fats to form lipofuscin. Animals deprived of vitamin E accumulate lipofuscin in their neurons at a much more rapid rate than those given adequate doses of the vitamin. This leads many scientists to believe that E is essential to proper brain function.

Although it is too early to tell for sure, it seems likely that vitamin E should at least slow down the deposition of lipofuscin. Older people should therefore make sure that they take in at least 50-100 IUs of vitamin E in their diet every day, from wheat germ, soybeans, broccoli, Brussels sprouts, leafy green vegetables, spinach, whole wheat bread, and whole grain cereals. If memory problems are present, it might be worth trying a heavier supplement. Up to 1000 IUs of E is perfectly safe, but it is always best to check with your doctor first before taking any more than 100 IUs daily.

Environment and Diet

The most common problems faced by the elderly do not include senility—they are a lack of environmental stimulation and a poor diet. Often, they go hand in hand. The person who sits at home most of the time, has few friends, rarely travels or goes out, and has no hobbies or interests is often also negligent about what he or she eats. The brain needs a balanced diet and environmental stimulation every day to stay in peak form. Just as stimulation plays a leading part in brain development, it also has a lot to do with slowing down brain deterioration. Failure to keep the mind busy is probably the most frequent cause of what is erroneously called "senility."

Older people must be encouraged to use their minds and remain active at all times. They also must be encouraged to eat regular meals. An older person may have a lot of valid reasons for not wanting to eat. Loneliness, the reduction of clear vision in older age (called presbyopia, or farsightedness due to the loss of elasticity in the crystalline lens of the eye), digestive disorders, the loss of taste acuity, gum problems, or just plain forgetfulness are all common reasons for skipping meals or for eating too little of what is nutritious and/or too much of what are just empty calories.

Life has much to offer at any age. Older people, or those who care about them, must make sure they are getting the most out of life by using their minds and by eating balanced, healthy meals.

How to Cope

To improve digestion:
- eat roughage: bran, whole wheat bread, grains, vegetables

To increase your sense of taste:
- zinc: 15 mg. supplement taken daily

If you have dental problems:
- eat softer foods, prepared in a more easily consumed fashion

To slow down rapid aging:
- cut down animal protein eaten

To control arteriosclerosis:
- cut out cholesterol
- eat pectin, found in apples, and citrus fruit
- eat fish
- eat a 1:1 ratio of animal to vegetable fat
- exercise

If you are anemic:
- eat red meat at least twice a week or liver once a week
OR
- iron: 10 mg. daily supplement, taken with meal
- folic acid: 400 mcg. daily supplement
- vitamin B_{12}: 6 mcg. daily supplement

BRAINFOOD

To improve your memory and energy, and to reduce feelings of confusion, disorientation, and paranoia:
- diet should contain RDA of iron (18 mg.), vitamin B_1 (1.5 mg.), and B_{12} (3 mcg.)
- cut down on alcohol
- don't use aluminum pans or utensils
- lecithin (phosphatidylcholine): 25-30 gram daily supplement

To reduce the effects of Parkinson's disease:
- See your doctor for levodopa (L-DOPA) treatment. Adjust dosage according to amount of protein consumed (the more protein, the more medicine). The lowest dosage should be achieved with a protein intake of 2-1/2 grams per 11 pounds of body weight.
- increase salt (check with your doctor)
- do *not* take tryptophan, tyrosine, or vitamin B_6 supplements

To fall asleep:
- tryptophan: 2-3 grams before bed with a carbohydrate snack

To raise your mood:
- tryptophan: 2-3 grams

To improve your memory:
- lecithin: 30 grams
- vitamin E: 100-1000 IU (check with your doctor for best dosage)

Appendices

APPENDIX 1

HOW THE DRUGS YOU TAKE CAN AFFECT YOUR BRAIN

Susan, a young legal secretary, had been suffering from stomach pains for almost a year. She finally saw her doctor, who diagnosed gastric hyperacidity and the beginnings of a duodenal ulcer. He prescribed the drug Tagamet (generic name: cimetidine), and in less than a month Susan was feeling much better.

Susan took Tagamet for three months. She ate the way she normally did, avoiding red meat as much as possible—partly because she didn't like its taste and also because she had found it hard to digest before being treated for her stomach problems. But new problems began to plague Susan. She was having trouble concentrating at work, found herself becoming increasingly irritable, and had frequent, severe headaches.

When Susan went back to her doctor and described her new symptoms, he asked about her diet and, discovering the lack of red meat, took a blood test. Susan was anemic, because the Tagamet had robbed her body of iron that she was not replacing through her meals. Tagamet, her doctor explained, could easily cause iron deficiency, because by preventing acid secretion in the stomach, it impairs the absorption of iron from vegetables (called ionic iron). The iron absorbed from meat (heme iron) would not be affected—but Susan wasn't getting any of that type. Her doctor recommended an iron supplement and told her to try and eat more red meat. The treatment was successful, and now Susan was rid of both stomach and mental disturbances.

Susan was one of the many people who do not realize that commonly used drugs (both prescription and over the counter) can upset the nutrient balance of the body in many different ways. Since we have seen that the brain needs particular nutrients for normal functioning, any disturbance in this area can also cause a corresponding problem in brain chemistry and function.

It is only in recent years that we have discovered how most of the drugs we take alter the way in which our bodies handle essential nutrients, which can lead to drug-induced nutrient deficiencies.

Food Absorption and Nutrient Metabolism

Many drugs either directly impair the absorption of nutrients, or increase the body's need for a nutrient by causing the body to use it inefficiently. A drug that interferes with the normal job of a given nutrient could cause all the signs and symptoms of a deficiency, the same signs one would see if the nutrient was completely missing from the diet. Other types of drugs simply cause you to excrete essential nutrients through the urine at a faster rate than normal. Finally, drugs can increase the body's need for certain nutrients by speeding up the internal processes that use such nutrients.

Mineral oil is a good example of how a drug can directly affect the absorption of food substances. This common laxative causes the malabsorption of the fat-soluble vitamins—A, D, E, and K—by imposing a physical barrier between the vitamins and the wall of the intestines (where these nutrients are normally absorbed). Denied absorption through the intestine, the vitamins simply dissolve in the nonabsorbable mineral oil. As captured nutrients, they are passed through the intestines and out the stool. If this laxative is abused (as is often the case with the elderly) by being used too frequently, a deficiency in one or more of these vitamins can result, leading to depression, apathy, and muscular spasms as a direct consequence of the deficiency.

Most interactions between drugs and nutrients are, however, more complex. The drug triamterene (Dyazide) is a commonly prescribed diuretic. This drug is an enemy of folic acid, as it prevents the nutrient from being converted into its active, usable form. If this drug is taken over an extended period of time, or in doses higher than 25 mg. daily, a deficiency in folic acid is likely to result, causing forgetfulness, apathy, irritability, insomnia, and depression.

Many minerals can be stripped from the body when a drug causes the kidneys to excrete them in abnormally large amounts. Diuretics, used to combat hypertension or water retention, are good examples of such drugs. They reduce the body's water content, as well as its salt (or sodium) content. However, they can also deplete the body of potassium, which is essential for nerve conduction. A deficiency would lead to such symptoms as anorexia, nausea, listlessness, and apprehension.

Oral contraceptives pose a particular problem. The estrogen they contain speeds up many reactions in the body that use riboflavin and vitamin B_6, thereby increasing the body's need for these vitamins. Estrogen also reduces the body's absorption of folic acid and vitamin B_{12}, as well as increasing the rate of degradation (and hence, the need for) vitamin C. Deficiencies and their accompanying symptoms can arise in any of these nutrients, especially in women who do not have a particularly good diet in the first place. Such deficiencies are believed to be at least partially responsible for the depression and irritability experienced by many women who take the pill.

Who Is at Risk?

Table 4 on p. 29 lists the "high-risk groups" for deficiencies in each vitamin and mineral. This will give you a comprehensive picture of whether you are in any vulnerable position(s). The chart of Drug-Nutrient Interactions on pp. 169-179 lists some commonly used drugs and the problems they can cause. If a drug you are taking is not listed there, it is best to consult with your physician and let him or her decide whether you actually need to take a supplement or should just eat more foods that are rich in the endangered nutrient.

Not everyone is at the same risk for a drug-induced nutrient deficiency. We all handle drugs and nutrients differently. However, the special nutritional requirements of the following groups make them particularly vulnerable to side effects:

- the elderly
- women in general, but especially those who are pregnant, lactating, or have reached menopause
- vegetarians
- heavy drinkers
- teenagers
- people on a severe weight loss, low-protein diet
- diabetics
- hypoglycemics
- children

Smokers, too, tend to have special nutritional requirements. They usually have lower blood levels of vitamins B_6 and B_{12}, which can indicate an increased need for these nutrients. It has been estimated that smokers also need up to one-and-a-half times the vitamin C required by nonsmokers, bringing the smoker's daily requirement up to 90 to 100 mg. a day. Smoking also tends to deplete the body of calcium.

In other words, everyone, but especially members of these high-risk groups, should be aware of all the nutritional consequences presented by the drugs they are taking. The health of both body and mind is at stake.

DRUG-NUTRIENT INTERACTIONS

This is a list of drugs, taken from the 200 most widely prescribed medications in America (including commonly used over-the counter drugs), which can drain the body of nutrients essential to proper brain function. To understand the effects on the brain of the nutrient deficiencies cited, see Table 4 on p. 29. In the case of iron and potassium, we have not given a dosage level for these substances, as they can be dangerous if taken in the wrong quantities. They should be administered by a physician.

DRUG	GENERIC NAME	PRESCRIBED FOR
Dyazide	triamterene	hypertension water retention
Phenobarbital Donnatal	phenobarbital	sedative anticonvulsant duodenal ulcer colitis
Penicillin VK Ledercillin VK Pfizerpen VK Pen-Vee-K V-cillin K	penicillin	antibiotic
Darvon Compound-65 Fiorinal—Codeine** Fiorinal Synalgos-DC	caffeine	pain relief tension headache
Fiorinal-Codeine Fiorinal Butisol-Sodium	barbiturate	pain relief tension headache
Septra Septra DS Bactrim DS	trimethoprim	antibiotic
Tegretol	carbamazepine	anticonvulsant and analgesic
Aldactone Aldactazide	spironolactone	water retention
Minocin Vibra-Tabs Vibramycin Tetracycline Syst (P-D) Sumycin SK-Tetracycline Achromycin-V	tetracycline	antibiotic

* "food" refers to the foods rich in this nutrient.
** The brand name of a drug may be repeated more than once, since many drugs contain combinations of generic drugs and it is the generic chemical that has the effect—and these effects differ according to the generic being discussed.

DEFICIENCY	SUPPLEMENT/FOOD
calcium	1000 mg. and food* (Table 6)
folic acid	food table (Table 25)
folic acid	400 mcg. and food (Table 25)
vitamin B_{12}	6 mcg. or food (Table 24)
vitamin D	400 IUs (Table 4)
vitamin K	100 mcg. and food (Table 4)
vitamin B_6	5 mg. or food (Table 14)
vitamin K	food (Table 4)
folic acid	food (Table 25)
vitamin B_6	5 mg. or food (Table 14)
vitamin B_{12}	6 mcg. or food (Table 4)
potassium	food (Table 7)
iron	food (or prescribe supplement (Table 17)
vitamin C	100 mg. or food (Table 4)
zinc	food (Table 24)
magnesium	food (Table 15)
folic acid	food (and 800 mcg. if more of the drug is taken) (Table 25)
dilution of blood sodium	restrict fluid intake to 6 glasses a day
calcium	1000 mg and food (Table 6)
riboflavin	5 mg. and food (Table 4)
vitamin C	100 mg. as food or supplement (Table 4)
folic acid	food (Table 25)
calcium	1000 mg. and food (Table 6)
iron	food (Table 17)
magnesium	food (Table 15)
zinc	food (Table 24)
vitamin B_6	5 mg. or food (Table 14)
vitamin B_{12}	5 mcg. or food (Table 4)

171

BRAINFOOD

DRUG	GENERIC NAME	PRESCRIBED FOR
Thorazine	chlorpromazine HCL	tranquilizer
Butazolidin	phenylbutazone	antiinflammatory
Ser-Ap-Es Inderide Enduron Hydropres Esidrix Aldoril Hydrodiuril Diuril Hygroton Dyazide Aldactazide	Thiazide diuretics	hypertension water retention
Equagesic Empirin-Codeine Fiorinal Fiorinal-Codeine Synalgos-DC Darvon Compound 65	aspirin	pain pain due to tension and anxiety
Dilantin	phenytoin	seizures
Indocin	indomethacin	arthritis
Eryc Erythromycin base syst. E. E. S. Ilosone Erythrocin E-Mycin 333 E-mycin Pediazole	erythromycin	antibiotic

DEFICIENCY	SUPPLEMENT/FOOD
riboflavin	food (Table 4)
raises cholesterol	reduce cholesterol intake in
levels	diet
iodine	food (Table 4)
potassium	food (Table 7)
zinc	food (Table 24)
magnesium	food (Table 15)
iodine	food (Table 4)
calcium	1000 mg. and food (Table 6)
iron	food (Table 23)
folic acid	food (Table 25)
vitamin C	100 mg. or food (Table 4)
vitamin B_1	food (Table 4)
vitamin K	food (Table 4)
vitamin K	100 mcg. and food (Table 4)
vitamin D	400 IUs and food (Table 4)
folic acid	800 mcg. and food (Table 25)
iron	food (Table 17)
folic acid	food (Table 25)
vitamin B_6	5 mg. and food (Table 14)
vitamin K	100 mcg. and food (Table 4)
vitamin B_{12}	6 mcg. or food (Table 4)
calcium	1000 mg. and food (Table 6)
magnesium	food (Table 15)

DRUG	GENERIC NAME	PRESCRIBED FOR
Tagamet	cimetidine	duodenal ulcer gastric hyper-acidity
Lanoxin	digoxin	cardiac insufficiency
Septra Bactrim DS Septra DS Pediazole	sulfamethoxazole	antibiotic
Coumadin	warfarin	prevention of blood clots
Ser-Ap-Es Apresoline	hydralazine	hypertension
Medrol Deltasone	corticosteroid	antiinflammatory
Aludrox Magnesium hydroxide Camalox Gelusil Kudrox Maalox Magnesia and Alumina Milk of Magnesia Mygel	magnesium antacid	gastric hyperacidity

DEFICIENCY	SUPPLEMENT/FOOD
iron	food (Table 17)
zinc	food (Table 24)
vitamin B_1	3 mg or food (Table 4)
magnesium	food (Table 15)
vitamin B_{12}	6 mcg. or food (Table 4)
folic acid	food (Table 25)
calcium	food (Table 6)
vitamin K	food (Table 4)
vitamin B_6	5 mg. or food (Table 14)
vitamin K	moderate amounts of food (Table 4)
vitamin B_6	food (Table 14) and 25 mg. to be taken 2-3 hours before taking the drug
calcium	1000 mg. and food (Table 6)
vitamin D	400 IUs and food (Table 4)
potassium	food (Table 7)
zinc	food (Table 24)
vitamin B_6	6 mg. or food (Table 14)
vitamin C	100 mg. or food (Table 4)
elevates blood cholesterol	limit cholesterol-rich foods (eggs, cheese, milk, red meat, animal fats)
calcium	food (Table 6)
phosphorus	food (Table 4)

DRUG	GENERIC NAME	PRESCRIBED FOR
Mylanta Simeco		
Alka-2 Biocal Cal-Sup Caltrate Camalox Marblen Os-Cal Philips' Lo-Sal Tempo Antacid Thermotabs Titralac Tums	calcium carbonate	supplement antacid
Oral contraceptives	estrogen	contraception
Premarin		menopause
Zyloprim	allopurinol	gout, cancer
Zinc sulfate	_____	supplement
Klotrix K-Lyte K-Tab	potassium	supplement
Camalox Delcid Di-Gel Gaviscon Gelusil Maalox Nephrax Tempo	aluminum antacids	gastric hyperacidity

DEFICIENCY	SUPPLEMENT/FOOD
phosphorus	food (Table 4)
magnesium	food (Table 15)
folic acid	400 mcg. and food (Table 25)
iron	food (Table 23)
vitamin B_1	2 mg. and food (Table 4)
riboflavin	food (Table 4)
folic acid	400 mcg. and food (Table 25)
vitamin B_6	5 mg. and food (Table 14)
vitamin B_{12}	6 mcg. or food (Table 4)
vitamin C	100 mg. and food (Table 4)
iron	food (Table 17)
copper	food (Table 4) or 3 mg. copper taken 2-3 hours before the zinc
vitamin B_{12}	6 mcg. or food (Table 4)
phosphorus	food (Table 4)
calcium	1000 mg. and food (Table 6)
magnesium	food (Table 15)
iron	food (Table 17)
vitamin A	food (Table 4) or multi-
vitamin C	food (Table 4) vitamin
vitamin D	food (Table 4) containing
vitamin B_1	food (Table 4) the RDA

DRUG	GENERIC NAME	PRESCRIBED FOR
Win-Gel		
Alterna Gel		
Aludrox		
Amphrojel		
Mylanta		
Simeco		
Ascriptin		
Kolantyl		
Magnatril		
Potassium Sodium Tartrate		laxative
Agoral	mineral oil	laxative
Ligni-Doss		
Milk of Magnesia		
Mineral Oil Emulsion		
Milkinol		
WhirtSol		
Olive Oil		laxative
Trilax	diphenylmethane	laxative
Bisacodyl		
Dulcolax		
Evac-Q-Kwik		
Phenolphthalein		
Agoral		
Evac-Q-Kit		
Evac-U-gen		
Pralet		
Sarolax		
Cascara	anthraquinone	laxative
Peri-Colace		
Danthron		
Doxidan		
Modane		
Senna		
Perdiem		
Senoket		
X-Prep		

DEFICIENCY	SUPPLEMENT/FOOD
folic acid	food (Table 25)
calcium	1000 mg. and food (Table 6)
vitamin D	400 IUs and food (Table 4)
vitamin K	100 mcg. and food (Table 4)
vitamin A	5000 IUs and food (Table 4)
potassium	food (Table 7)
calcium	1000 mg. and food (Table 6)
iron	food
potassium	food (Table 7)
vitamin D	400 IUs and food (Table 4)
calcium	1000 mg. and food (Table 6)
potassium	food (Table 7)

179

STRUCTURE AND FUNCTION OF THE BRAIN

HINDBRAIN OR BRAINSTEM

Medulla Oblongata: Responsible for receiving taste sensations; sends signals to help work muscles of speech; helps regulate breathing, heartbeat, blood pressure, and digestion; responsible for operating the muscles of the neck and back that turn the head and shoulders; controls movements of poking out tongue and using tongue in speech; controls coughing, swallowing, sneezing, and gagging.

Pons: Receives sensations from facial skin and from the eyes, nose, mouth, and teeth (i.e., "runny" nose, dry eyes, toothache); tells the jaw muscles to chew; controls the outer muscle of the eye that moves eye to the side; receives sensations of taste from the front of the tongue; works the muscles that control facial expressions; receives nerve impulses from sounds entering the ear, enabling hearing; receives signals from the cochlea, a balance organ in the ear; causes secretion of saliva and tears.

Midbrain: Works five of the six muscles that move the eye and the muscle that controls the size and reactions of the pupil; helps maintain balance; receives information about positioning of muscles around the eyes and jaw.

Reticular Formation: Group of nerve fibers deep in the brain running from the medulla oblongata to the midbrain. Receives information from every part of the body and sends it to cells in the hypothalamus, cerebral cortex, cerebellum and spinal cord, and in this way governing the level of activity of the entire nervous system. When you are inactive there is little activity here; when you awake activity takes a dramatic upswing.

CEREBELLUM

Helps maintain posture and adjusts muscle movements; its signals modify direction, rate, force, and steadiness of quick, intentional movements; the source of muscle memory or physical intelligence, making learned movements, such as walking or serving a tennis ball, automatic.

DIENCEPHALON

Area deep in the forebrain between the brainstem and cerebral hemispheres.

Thalamus: Major integrator of information flowing in from the sensory organs to the cerebral cortex. All sensory signals pass this way. The two thalami ("deep chambers") receive information fed in from the body via the spinal cord and receive input from the eyes and ears. After analyzing signals, it speeds each different type off to specific areas of the cerebral cortex. Affects long-term memory.

Hypothalamus: Lies under the thalamus. Although smaller than a fingertip and weighing only a quarter-ounce, it performs more tasks than any other brain structure of comparable size. Regulates body temperature; controls thirst and appetite; influences blood pressure, sexual behavior, aggression, fear, and sleep; communicates with the limbic system; controls the pituitary gland.

Pituitary Gland: Leader of the endocrine orchestra, produces hormones influencing other glands that regulate vital body activities. Its hormones affect growth, sexual development, the conversion of food into energy; regulate urine output (helping to conserve body water); influence milk production and the production of oxytocin (which regulates the contractions of the uterus during childbirth).

Pineal Gland: Light-sensitive clock that affects sleep and the sex glands.

THE BASAL GANGLIA

Help to handle physical movements by relaying information from the cerebral cortex to the brainstem and cerebellum. Also seem to be responsible for some muscle memory. They relay information to cerebral cortex before a well-known movement (walking, for example) is made.

THE LIMBIC SYSTEM

Handles emotions; is involved in the acquisition of new information, or short-term memory. Impulses are passed through limbic system's internal pathways and onto other forebrain regions and the cerebellum. Triggered or modulated by these signals, limbic structures arouse or temper feelings that range from joy to misery, love to hate.

THE CEREBRAL CORTEX

Motor Cortex: Extends from ear to ear across the roof of the brain and exercises control over the muscles.

Premotor Cortex: Strip of cortex just in front of the motor cortex, which it controls. It plans the reactions of the motor cortex to a specific type of stimuli in light of past experience.

Occipital Lobes: Deal with all matters of vision, including short-term memory for visual phenomena.

Parietal Lobes: Regulate special perception; contain short-term memory for the perception of motion.

Prefrontal Lobes: Determine a person's response to circumstances—responses may range from despair, anxiety, and dislike to ecstasy, optimism, and delight. Not involved with intellect. Damage to this area makes a person passive, with fewer extremes of emotional responses.

Sensory Cortex: Strip of cortex parallel to the motor cortex, handling awareness of bodily sensations (i.e., hot vs. cold, wet vs. dry). Enables us to distinguish between one face and another.

Temporal Lobes: Handle ability to interpret speech, and regulate long- and short-term memory.

Hippocampus: Regulates short- and long-term memory; controls emotions.

Frontal Lobes: Deal with matters of intellect and creativity. The main storage sites for long-term memory.

THE SPINAL CORD

Carries neurons (nerve cells) that connect the body to the neurons in the brain, and vice versa.

CEREBROSPINAL FLUID

Watery fluid produced in the four linked cavities (ventricles) inside the brain. The fluid fills these cavities and flows, via special ducts, around the brain's outer rim before being reabsorbed into the blood. Thus the brain floats in a bath that may effectively reduce its weight 20 times, the way a person becomes "lighter" when swimming in a pool. This surrounding fluid acts as a cushion to buffer the brain against shock and makes turning or nodding the head an effortless act instead of excruciating torment. Cerebrospinal fluid also protects the spinal cord, in fact, 1/5 of it lies in the brain and 4/5 lies in the spinal cord.

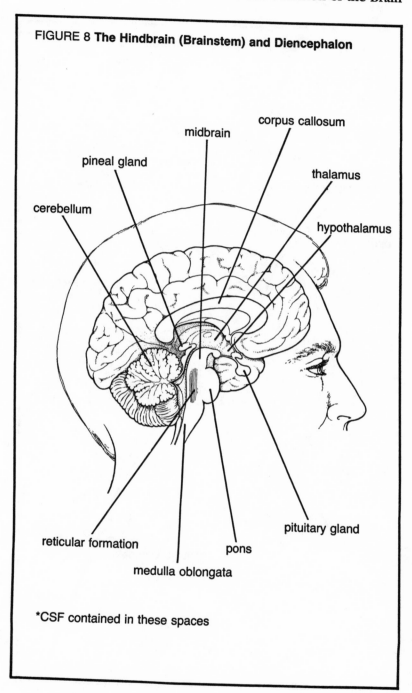

FIGURE 8 **The Hindbrain (Brainstem) and Diencephalon**

corpus callosum

midbrain

thalamus

pineal gland

hypothalamus

cerebellum

reticular formation

pons

pituitary gland

medulla oblongata

*CSF contained in these spaces

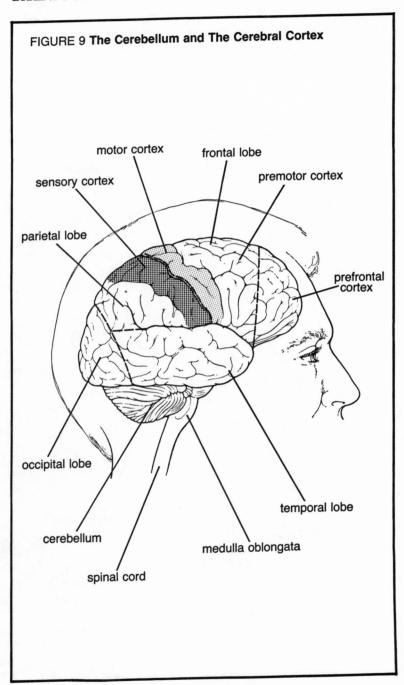

FIGURE 9 **The Cerebellum and The Cerebral Cortex**

motor cortex

frontal lobe

sensory cortex

premotor cortex

parietal lobe

prefrontal cortex

occipital lobe

temporal lobe

cerebellum

medulla oblongata

spinal cord

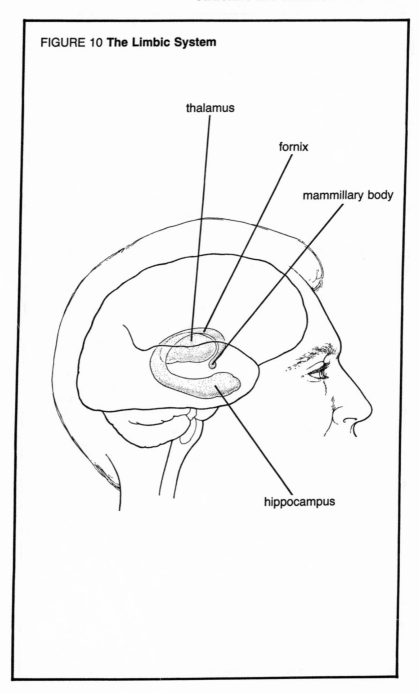

FIGURE 10 **The Limbic System**

thalamus

fornix

mammillary body

hippocampus

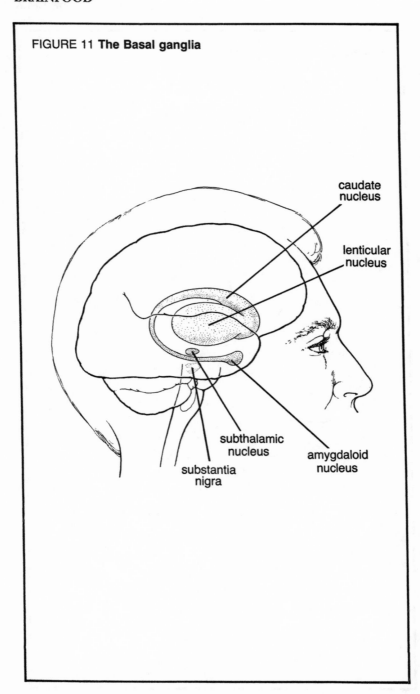

FIGURE 11 **The Basal ganglia**

caudate nucleus

lenticular nucleus

subthalamic nucleus

amygdaloid nucleus

substantia nigra

REFERENCES

Richard Wurtman, "Behavioral Effects of Nutrients," *Lancet,*
May 21, 1983, pp. 1145-47

Jean A. T. Pennington and Helen Nichols Church, *Bowes and
Church's Food Values of Portions Commonly Used,* J. B.
Lippincott Co., Philadelphia, 1985

The British Medical Association and the Pharmaceutical Society of Great Britain, *British National Formulary,* London,
1984

Judith J. Wurtman, Richard J. Wurtman, John W. Growdon,
Peter Henry, Anne Lipscomb and Steven H. Zeisel, "Carbohydrate Cravings in Obese People: Suppression by Treatments Affecting Serotoninergic Transmission," *International Journal of Eating Disorders,* vol. 1, no. 1, pp.
2-11, 1981

N. Sitaram, Herbert Weingartner, Eric D. Caine and J. Christian
Gillin, "Choline: Selective Enhancement of Serial Learning
and Encoding of Low Imagery Words in Man," *Life Sciences,*
vol. 22, p. 1555-60, 1978

Judith Wurtman, Richard Wurtman, Sharon Mark, Rita Tsay,
William Gilbert and John Growdon, "d-Fenfluramine Selectively Suppresses Carbohydrate Snacking by Obese Subjects," *International Journal of Eating Disorders,* vol. 4, no.
1, pp. 89-99, 1985

Peter D. Leathwood and Patricia Pollet, "Diet-Induced Mood Changes in Normal Populations," *Journal of Psychiatric Research,* vol. 17, no. 2, pp. 147-154, 1982/83

Ernest Hartman, "Effect of L-Tryptophan on Sleepiness and on Sleep," *Journal of Psychiatric Research,* vol. 17, no. 2, pp. 107-13, 1982/83

Bonnie Spring, Owen Maller, Judith Wurtman, Larry Digman and Louis Cozolino, "Effects of Protein and Carbohydrate Meals on Mood and Performance: Interactions with Sex and Age," *Journal of Psychiatric Research,* vol. 17, no. 2, pp. 155-67, 1982/83

Ernesto Pollitt, Nita L. lewis, Cuthberto Garza and Robert J. Shulman, "Fasting and Cognitive Function," *Journal of Psychiatric Research,* vol. 17, no. 2, pp. 169-74, 1982/83

G. P. Smith and J. Gibbs, "Gut Peptides and Postprandial Satiety," *Federation Proc.,* vol. 43, pp. 2889-92, 1984

A. A. Paul and D. A. T. Southgate, *McCance and Widdowson's The Composition of Foods,* Her Majesty's Stationery Office, London, 1978

G. Hopkinson, "Mood and Appetite," *Journal of Obesity and Weight Regulation,* vol. 4, no. 1, pp. 50-56, 1985

Harris R. Lieberman, Suzanne Corkin, Bonnie J. Spring, John H. Growdon and Richard J. Wurtman, "Mood, Performance and Pain Sensitivity: Changes Induced by Food Constituents," *Journal of Psychiatric Research,* vol. 17, no. 2, pp. 135-45, 1982/83

Hendrik Lehnert, Daniel K. Reinstein, Benjamin W. Strowbridge and Richard J. Wurtman, "Neurochemical and Behavioral Consequences of Acute, Uncontrollable Stress: Effects of Dietary Tyrosine," *Brain Research,* vol. 303, pp. 215-23, 1984

John E. Morley, Allen S. Levine, Blake A. Gosnell, Charles J. Billington, "Neuropeptides and Appetite: Contribution of Neuropharmacological Modeling," *Federation Proc.,* vol. 43, pp. 2903-07, 1984

Richard J. Wurtman and Judith J. Wurtman, eds. *Nutrition and the Brain: Determinants of the Availability of Nutrients to the Brain,* vol. 1, Raven Press, New York, 1977

References

Nutrition and the Brain: Control of Feeding Behavior and Biology of the Brain in Protein-Calorie Malnutrition, vol. 2, Raven Press, New York, 1977

Nutrition and the Brain: Disorders of Eating—Nutrients in Treatment of Brain Diseases, vol. 3, Raven Press, New York, 1979

Nutrition and the Brain: Toxic Effects of Food Constituents on the Brain, vol. 4, Raven Press, New York, 1979

Andre Barbeau, John W. Growdon and Richard J. Wurtman, eds., *Nutrition and the Brain: Choline and Lecithin in Brain Disorders,* vol. 5, Raven Press, New York, 1979

Richard J. Wurtman and Judith J. Wurtman, eds., *Nutrition and the Brain: Physiological and Behavioral Effects of Food Constituents,* vol. 6, Raven Press, New York, 1983

George K. W. Yim and Martin T. Lowy, "Opiods, Feeding and Anorexia," *Federation Proc.,* vol. 43, pp. 2893-97, 1984

Frank Winston, "Oral Contraceptives, Pyridoxine and Depression," *American Journal of Psychiatry,* vol. 130, no. 11, pp. 1217-21, 1973

Roger C. Duvois, *Parkinson's Disease: a Guide for Patient and Family,* Raven Press, New York, 1984

Brian L. G. Morgan and Myron Winick, "Pathologic Effects of Malnutrition on the Central Nervous System," in Herschel Sidransky, ed., *Nutrition Pathology: Pathobiochemistry of Dietary Imbalances,* Marcel Dekker, Inc., New York, 1985

Eric R. Kandel and James H. Schwarz, *Principles of Neural Science,* Elsevier/North-Holland, Oxford 1983

Arthur Yuwiler, Gary L. Brammer, John E. Morley, Michael J. Raleigh, Jeffry W. Flannery and Edward Geller, "Short-Term and Repetitive Administration of Oral Tryptophan in Normal Men," *Arch. of General Psychiatry,* vol. 38, pp. 619-25. 1981

Judith J. Wurtman and Richard J. Wurtman, "Studies on the Appetite for Carbohydrates in Rats and Humans," *Journal of Psychiatric Research,* vol. 17, no. 2, pp. 213-21, 1982/83

The Brain: a Scientific American Book, W. H. Freeman and Co., San Francisco, 1979

Samuel Seltzer, Dorothy Dewart, Robert L. Pollack and Eric Jackson, "The Effects of Dietary Tryptophan on Chronic Maxillofacial Pain and Experimental Pain Tolerance," *Jour-*

nal of Psychiatric Research, vol. 17, no. 2, pp. 181-86, 1982/83

Brian L. G. Morgan, *The Food and Drug Interaction Guide,* Simon and Schuster, New York, 1986

Brian L. G. Morgan, *The Lifelong Nutrition Guide,* Prentice-Hall, Inc., Englewood Cliffs, 1983

Alan J. Gelenberg, Joanne D. Wojcik, Candance J. Gibson and Richard J. Wurtman, "Tryosine for Depression," *Journal of Psychiatric Research,* vol. 17, no. 2, pp. 175-80. 1982/83

INDEX